Contemporary Craft

THE SOURCEBOOK FOR COLLECTORS & GALLERIES

3

Published by
THE GUILD
931 E. Main Street #106
Madison, WI 53703-2954
http://www.guild.com
TEL 800-969-1556
TEL 608-256-1990
FAX 608-256-1938

Administration
Toni Fountain Sikes, President
James F. Black, Jr., Vice President · Susan K. Evans, Vice President
Tom Christensen, Sales Manager · Theresa Ace, Business Manager
Deb Lovelace, Operations Manager · Emily Lovelace, Administrative Assistant

Production, Design, Editorial
Cheryll Mellenthin, Production Manager · Marcia LaCour-Little, Production Assistant
Katie Kazan, Editorial Manager · Theodora Zehner, Editorial Assistant
Leslie Ferrin, Writer · Karen Thuermer, Writer

Thanks to the American Craft Council/American Craft Enterprises for permission to reprint the "Glossary of Craft Terms"
Printed by Four Colour Imports, Ltd., Louisville, KY

Publisher's Representatives
Tom Christensen · Susan K. Evans
Martha Johnson · Diane Nelson
Karen O. Brown · William N. Fortescue

THE GUILD JAPAN
Yuko Yokoyama, Jomon-sha

North American Distribution
Watson-Guptill Publications
a division of BPI Communications, Inc.
1515 Broadway
New York, NY 10036

Special thanks to our 1996 Review Committee
Leslie Ferrin, The Ferrin Gallery
Fredda Harris, CrossHarris Fine Crafts
Tara Silberberg, The Clay Pot

Cover Art
Angsoka, by Andiamo Glass Design, 1995, blown glass, etched, painted and cased, 12"H x 11"W
photo: Robert Spielholz. See page 57.

⠿ THE GUILD⠄
is a registered trademark of Kraus Sikes Inc.

ISBN (softback) 1-880140-20-9
ISBN (hardback) 1-880140-19-5

Printed in Hong Kong

Contemporary Craft

THE SOURCEBOOK FOR COLLECTORS & GALLERIES

3

::: THE GUILD®

Kraus Sikes Inc.
Madison, Wisconsin
USA

Table of Contents

In Their Own Words

It's clichéd, perhaps, to speak of the artist's singular vision or unique lifestyle. This short scrapbook of images and observations from our featured artists is nontheless fresh and engaging, a privileged look behind the studio wall.

Building a Craft Collection

Collecting contemporary craft is an exercise of heart and mind, and a bit of guidance can make a big difference. In this essay, gallery owner Leslie Ferrin takes imaginary clients through the predictable seasons of a collection, offering wise counsel along the way.

Finding the Artwork

The beautiful artwork shown in this book is as close as your telephone — or perhaps your local gallery. Look here to find direct phone numbers for *Contemporary Craft* artists — and the galleries which carry their work.

Listing of Galleries By State

All galleries on this state-by-state listing display the artwork of Contemporary Craft artists. The list is a great travel companion, and may introduce fine outlets in your own backyard.

Selected Publications and Organizations

A few of these resources focus on the decorative arts as a whole; most are media-specific. All provide outstanding information about artists, materials, techniques and exhibitions.

Index of Artists and Companies

Can't find an artist? With both personal and company names for every artist, our index is the place to look.

Table of Contents

Featured Artists
A gorgeous gallery of handmade objects and wearables.

Publisher's Note

This third edition of Contemporary Craft presents an astound-
ing array of creative expressions by some of the top artists in
the field. The skill involved in making this work is, in itself,
astonishing. But we wanted to know more. How do these men
and women make these incredible things? Why do they do
what they do? What are the stories behind the work?

To find the answers, we asked the artists themselves. They
responded in thoughtful, insightful, quirky and (to be
expected) totally creative ways.

Throughout this book you will find, in their own words, scrapbook self-portraits, fragments of explanation and illumination.
We hope our explorations provide a richer context in which to
view these objects of beauty and delight.

Toni Fountain Sikes
Publisher

A CLARITY OF SPIRIT

Featured artists ... in their own words

**ARTISTS ARE, AMONG OTHER THINGS
EXQUISITE STORYTELLERS.**

They tell their stories in many forms, from the seemingly ageless clay pot brushed by fire, to the glass vessel gleaming like a jewel in the sun, to the elegant gold necklace that makes the wearer feel like a fairy princess.

These objects then become our preface. They speak to us; they move us. We take them home and live with the story and add our personal embellishments along the way.

The best objects come from the best stories, and the best stories grow out of the lives of the artists like roots grow a tree. Throughout the following pages are glimpses — in the artists' own words — into the way they work and live, and even some of the philosophy behind why they do what they do.

These words and phrases speak to the character of the storyteller: imaginative, adventurous, idealistic (though tempered with pragmatism). All in all, a clarity of spirit that inspires the best in all of us.

Keep in mind that the words and photos are only the faintest of whispers, hopefully enticing you to lean forward and listen a little harder. And they are offered in the best storytelling tradition: from the heart, with a hint of a smile.

Photo: Damayanti Joshee

" When I began working with weavers in Nepal in 1983, I was simply intent on turning my computer graphics into rugs. As the years passed and interest in my work grew, I was able to become more involved with those that I work with. It is a long arduous process to transform a picture into a rug, and there have been many times that I thought I might just throw in the towel. It is these wonderful human relationships that have kept things going.

Working in a Third World country such as Nepal raises many questions of accountability for me. In 1990, I began the process of building my own rug factory to be able to provide the kind of working and living conditions which I felt would offer my weavers a good quality of life. To that end, I provide housing, food, medical, above average pay, and I never employ children.

Today, weavers at the Contemporary Carpet Center have savings accounts, take vacations, raise families, and enjoy their work. When I thank someone for purchasing one of our rugs, I am thanking them both for their interest in my artwork and for the weavers whose patience and skilled hands produce these magical pieces. "

Carl T. Chew, rug designer
Seattle, WA

"To be an artist is to create light in a dark place, to put warmth in the cold, to stretch to a new dimension; it is to become. Fevers burn, dreams transform, souls commune, but all in their own time."

Betty Fulmer, sculptor
Findlay, OH

in their own words . . .

Alice: *"The experience of cancer in 1994 gave me an opportunity to deepen the content of my artwork. It now carries a gentle symbolism for the transformative power of challenges, and encourages dialogue which is healing for myself and others."*

HANDLE WITH BELIEF

©Alice Watterson

BACKGROUND: WOVEN THROW FROM JILL COLLIER DESIGNS, BRISTOL, RI, PHOTO: BOB BARRETT

"This is what I see when I look out of my studio window: The Tennessee mountains, ever changing with mist or clouds, leaves of green then gold or russet, bare branches, snow or rain, sunlight slanting from the east or west, and shadows, wonderful shadows climbing the eastern mountain at sunset. Sometimes it is a study in grays, and at night the moonlight lights the mountains with a delicate touch."

**Betty Kershner, fiber artist
Sewanee, TN**

Photos: Ivor Markman

Ann Corcoran (above) of the Nourot Glass Studio in Benicia, CA, with tools of their trade.

Nourot's clients have included Pope John Paul II, Hillary Rodham Clinton, and the World Figure Skater's Federation.

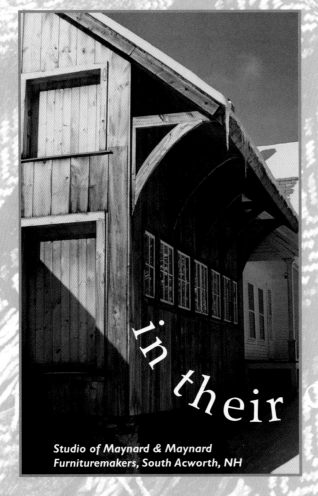

in their

*Studio of Maynard & Maynard
Furnituremakers, South Acworth, NH*

. . . own words

Q. Peter, why do you do what you do?
A. In this day and age, with such a rootless feeling in our culture, I am one of those people who have chosen to come to rest in a craft, in the hope of finding a kind of repose in my life.

PETER MAYNARD

in their own words . . .

"There is nothing mysterious about the work that I do. A vivid imagination, a little luck, lots of time and patience, a good working knowledge of wood and woodworking tools, and of course, a passion to create — that's all that it takes."

Richard Sheremeta

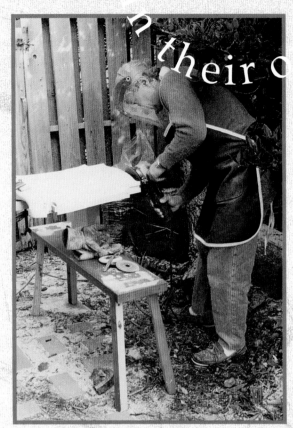

Richard Sheremeta, using an angle grinder to shape a rocking chair seat, outside his Delray Beach, FL, studio

"I'm not as good with words as I am with wood. The smiles on the children's faces say it all for me."

Russ Jacobsohn of Russ's Rural Rockers, Sparta, TN

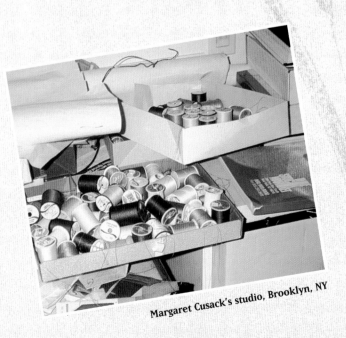

Margaret Cusack's studio, Brooklyn, NY

"The Northwest weather and culture have had a clear effect on our work. We love the forests and the beauty of nature around us, and these themes show up repeatedly in our work. I think our inclination to use intense, saturated and primary colors arises at least in part as a defense against Seattle s seemingly continuous winter gray."

Robert Spielholz and Kathleen Hargrave of Andiamo Glass Design, Redmond, WA

"I see my work speaking very directly to people about the trees, how they grow, the infinite variety within even a particular species. By letting the burls, a usually ignored deformity, remain their own shape, I hope to allow the tree itself to speak to the beholder. I look for what the burl wants to be, rather than apply my ideas to it. The intuitive steps are more analogous to listening or receiving than to speaking or telling."

Abby Morrison,
Rockland, ME

Abby Morrison

photo: Deb Soule

"Artistic hands ... Healing hands ... Creative hands ... One seems to blend into or reflect the next and with a gentle force that seems unstoppable. I have wondered many times 'what element makes them so?'

Being the fifth generation in a line of women who created things both practical and beautiful with their hands, perhaps I am 'genetically gifted', perhaps I don't have to think about it anymore, my hands just know."

Kira J. Maer-lyn, Madison, WI

"We are two very different artists, sharing a studio on the beach overlooking Long Island Sound. Our joint studio experience has been very rewarding, fostering a powerful friendship, as well as enhancing artistic development."

Deborah Sabo and
Alice Van de Wetering
Riverhead, NY

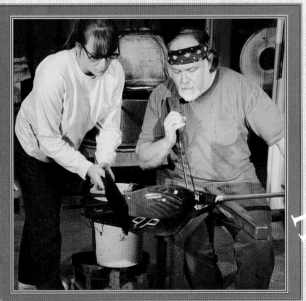

photo: Peregrin Spielholz

in their own words ...

11

Diane Hulet of Hulet Glass,
McKinleyville, CA, lampworking a marble

"About once a week I go out in the yard and
paint long sheets of copper. The rest of the time we
weave and build, design, pack and ship. But it's during those times of
painting, under the bright sun, in the back yard, that I feel transported
into another realm, as I watch the colors unfold and move across the metal.

I believe that somewhere, in some other world, the inhabitants speak in
colors. I'm trying to reach that place ... to speak, see, feel that speech,
and perhaps to bring a little of it back."

Suzanne Donazetti of Metalweavings, Carrizozo, NM
From Suzanne's notebook

Featured Artists

The visions and sentiments expressed in the
previous pages reflect the domino-chain of
lifestyle choices that are part of the artist's being.
Truly, the artist creates his or her own world
more thoroughly — and often in more colorful
detail — than the rest of us. The works of
art on the following pages are fragments
distilled from these worlds, offered to share.

JEWELRY JEWELRY

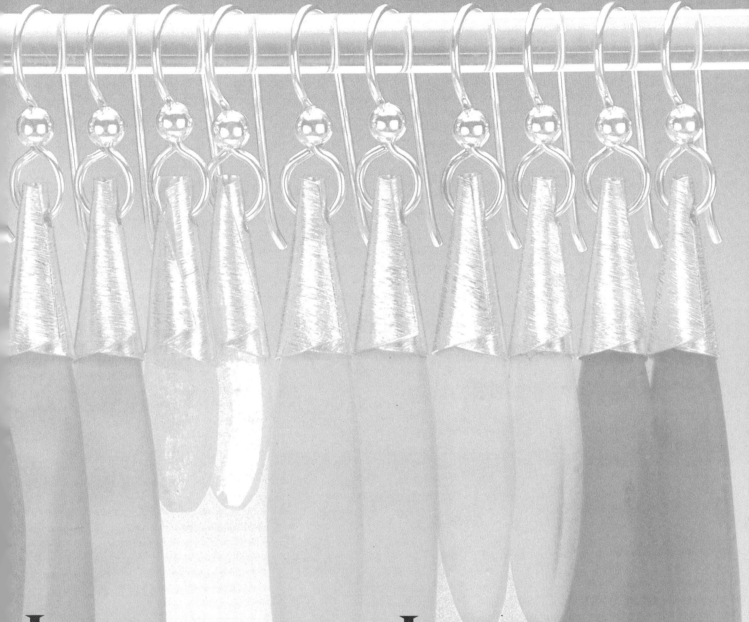

JEWELRY JEWELRY

Irena Stein

Irena Stein Ceramics

Irena Stein is a Venezuelan designer living in the San Francisco Bay area. She has designed ceramic jewelry since 1986.

Stein's limited-edition collection for galleries includes earrings, pins, cufflinks and pendants. These pieces are very light and made entirely by hand. They combine glazes and lusters to give the appearance that the work is a combination of metal and clay.

The collection is sold in Europe, Asia, and North and South America.

SHOWN: Pins and earrings, 1995, matte and semi-matte glazes with gold luster

George Post, Richmond, CA

George Post

Nancy Goodenough, Glass Artist

Nancy Goodenough

Nancy Goodenough's *Cosmic Craters* © series of glass jewelry is said to resemble 'opals from distant planets.'

The artist combines the ancient glass-forming technique of pâte de verre with her innovative manipulation of space-aged dichroic glass. Using diamond lapidary equipment, she bevels and shapes the glass into exceptional pendants, pins and earrings, some set in sterling.

Nancy Goodenough's distinctive jewelry is available in galleries across the United States, the world and the galaxy.

SHOWN: *Cosmic Craters* series, 1995, cast dichroic glass jewelry, ©Nancy Goodenough

Julie Shaw

Julie Shaw Designs Inc.

Julie Shaw intermingles natural minerals, the brilliance of precious and semi-precious stones, and the richness of 14K and 22K gold with sterling silver that has been oxidized to achieve wonderful purples, blues, and warm earthtones.

Julie Shaw's travels to the Mid- and Far-East, and her life experiences and connection to the land, are her inspiration.

You will be equally at home wearing Julie Shaw's jewelry on a casual afternoon or at an elegant affair.

Julie Shaw currently resides in southwest Colorado, with her studio overlooking the San Juan Mountains.

A Earrings, sterling silver, 14K gold, opal, smithsonite, rhodalite, garnet, pearls, each 2"L × ³/₄"W

B Brooch, sterling silver, 14K gold, opal, Colorado mineral, pearls, 3"L × 1¹/₄"W

A

B

Photos: Allen Bryan

Idelle Hammond-Sass Design

Idelle Hammond-Sass

Jewelry designer Idelle Hammond-Sass is equally at home creating her contemporary heirlooms in gold or silver. Metals are uniquely textured, combined and accented with pearls and gemstones. Her pieces are elegant, highly expressive and personal.

Idelle's award-winning jewelry can be found at select galleries, jewelry stores and craft fairs nationally.

SHOWN: Bracelet and earrings, ©1995, sterling silver and 14K gold with iolite, amethyst and tourmaline cabochons

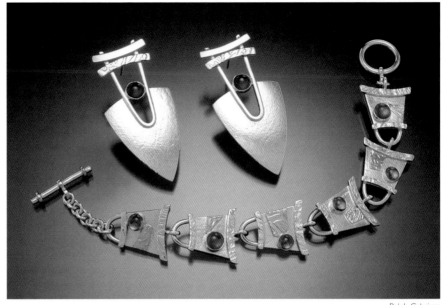

Ralph Gabriner

Ralph Gabriner

Alice Van de Wetering Designs

Alice Van de Wetering

Alice Van de Wetering's jewelry reflects her interest in primitive cultures: their symbols, rituals and traditions. The pieces are hand sawn, reticulated and riveted. Her work has been pictured in *American Craft* magazine and *Ornament*. She's exhibited in galleries nationally and in Finland and Czeckoslovakia.

SHOWN: Works in sterling: earrings with carnelian dangles; bracelet with assorted stones; larger pin with carved acrylic, shell bead, black coral

GB Jewelry
Sonia GutierrezBecher

Contemporary gold and sterling jewelry featuring creatively set, unique gemstones. Sonia's creations are one-of-a-kind. Color, texture and shape give each piece a character of its own. Her work is unified with the consistent use of the pillowed 'shell' for which she is renowned. The attention to detail given to the finishing and setting make each piece an absolute treasure.

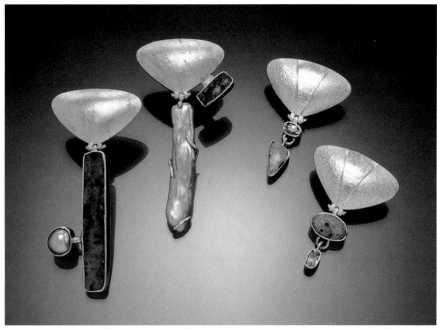

Asymmetrical earrings, 1995, sterling and 22K gold, left: opals and pearls, 2½"L × 1"W; right: opals, peridot and topaz, 1½"L × 1"W

Ralph Gabriner

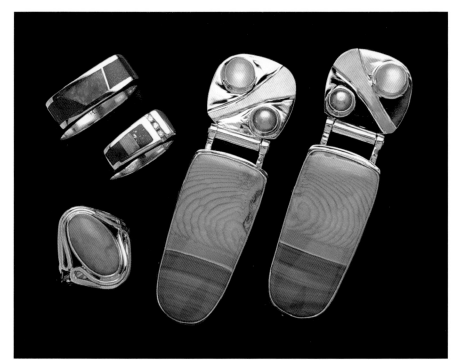

Jim Osterberg

The Harrington Collection, Ltd.
Neil Herman/Laura Herman

The Hermans' designs are clean, pure and simple. They use a blend of classic and contemporary styles that work well for any occasion and across generations.

They especially enjoy making people happy with the jewelry they make, by changing someone's outlook for a moment, a day, or a lifetime when they wear a piece created by The Harrington Collection, Ltd.

The Hermans love what they do and enjoy working with new and old customers.

Barbara Bayne

Barbara has been creating fine jewelry for more than seven years. Her work reflects her interest in the natural forms and textures which she has observed in nature. She seeks to capture some of that nature when creating bracelets, earrings, brooches and necklaces made of both 14K gold and sterling.

SHOWN: Bracelet, earrings and pendant, 1995, 14K gold and sterling; bracelet: 7" × ½" × ¼"; earrings: 1" × ⅜" × ¼"; pendant: ¾" × 2⅜" × ½"

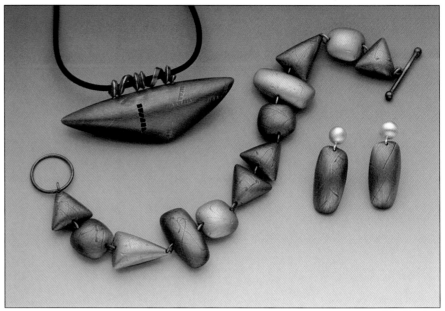

Peter Groesbeck

Myers Gondek Design

The collection of jewelry created by Rebecca Myers and Mark Gondek reflects their love of texture, pattern and color. The use of high karat gold, combined with varied surface treatments such as embossing, chasing and inlay, is indicative of the ancient Egyptian work from which they draw. The attention paid to details such as tiny hinges and beaded edges (often surrounding a boulder opal) enhances the look of each piece.

SHOWN: *Egyptian Series*, 1995, earrings, ring, pearl enhancer, sterling silver with 18K white and yellow gold, 22K gold overlay, boulder opal, rhodolite garnet, Chinese freshwater pearls

Elizabeth Prior

The unique process of soldering 18K and 14K gold to entirely hand-built sterling silver allows this jewelry to be substantial in size and appearance at a less-than-prohibitive price.

While particularly intrigued by what metal can do, Elizabeth Prior also uses a number of semi-precious cabachons as color accents. Her strong design sense and formal fine-art background make each piece a personal statement that carries a sense of history in a contemporary look.

Ms. Prior's work has been represented by museum stores and galleries throughout the United States since 1988. In 1995, *Jeweler's Circular Keystone* named her one of seven 'Rising Stars' in the fine-jewelry industry.

SHOWN: Nine pins and one earring, 18K gold and sterling silver with 14 and 18K gold appliqué, shown actual size

Jon Bonjour

Jan D. Gjaltema

Influenced by his education and experience in architecture, Dutch-born Jan D. Gjaltema (1951) combines the linear and structural with the modern and forward look to produce a most varied and distinctive collection of handcrafted sterling jewelry for both men and women. He is represented by some of the finest galleries in Europe and the United States.

Jan does not show his work at any craft or trade show in the U.S. or abroad. His work is not sold through representatives. Serious inquiries by mail only.

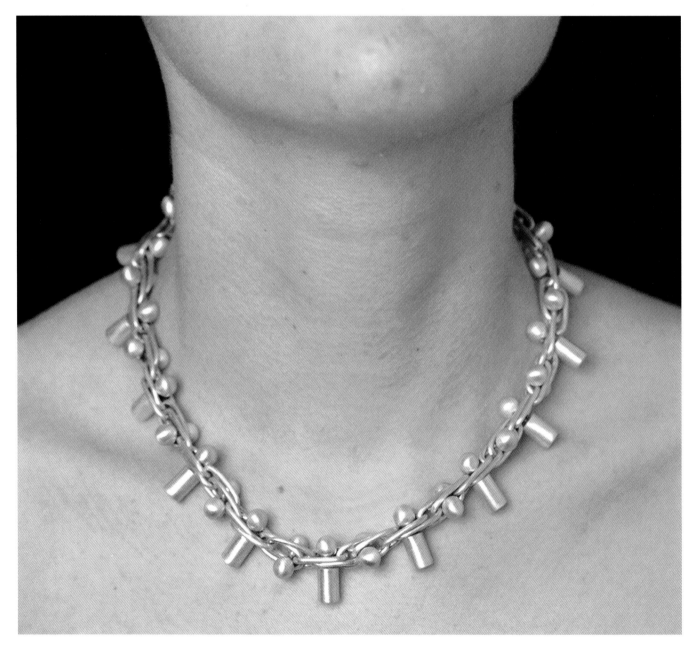

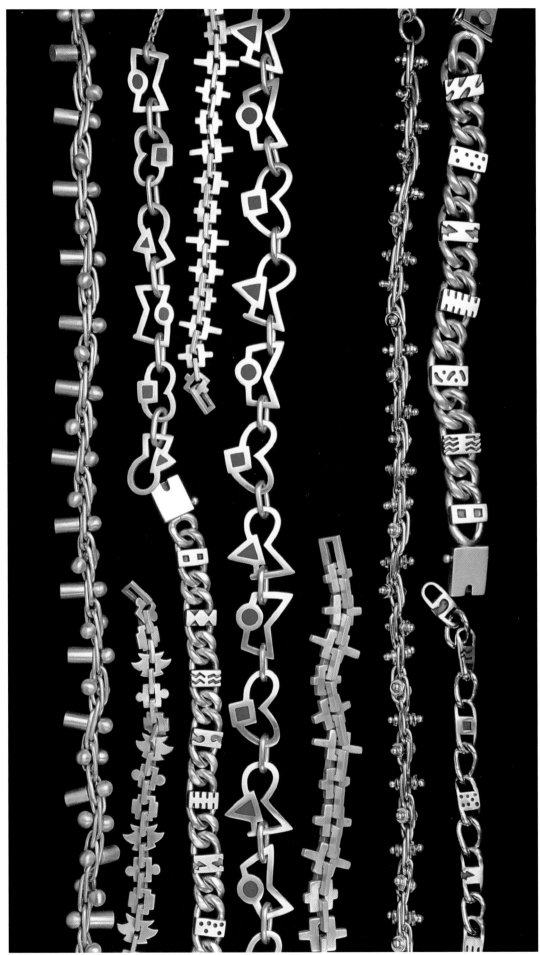

Jan D. Gjaltema

Stevi Belle
Winged Woman Creations

Stevi Belle has been working with glass for seven years. Her experience ranges from glass blowing to cast and fused glass to her current work on the torch. Currently her work expresses two distinct styles, one being a very contemporary bead that she calls her asteroid series and the other a study of ancient vessel forms that often appear to represent goddess figures. All of her glass beads are lampwound and one of a kind. She also does sculptural pieces that are 'goddess staffs.'

A *Asteroid Necklace*, 1995, glass, silver, copper, 26"L, largest bead 1¼"Dia

B *Ancient Vessel*, 1995, glass, copper, 3"L

C *Goddess Pendant*, 1995, glass, copper, gold, 1995, 3⅛"L

D *Ancient Vessel*, 1995, glass, copper, 3⅛"L

A

B

C

D

Photos: Jerry Anthony, Columbus, OH

Zoë Pasternack

ZoëBella

Softly frosted glass earrings and necklaces by Zoë Pasternack are reminiscent of sea-glass tumbled in sand and washed up on the shore. Zoë creates a clean, contemporary look which showcases the vibrant, luminous qualities of the glass.

Set with sterling silver, patinated brass or freshwater pearls, and conceived in a palette of pastels and brights, the designs joyfully complement any style.

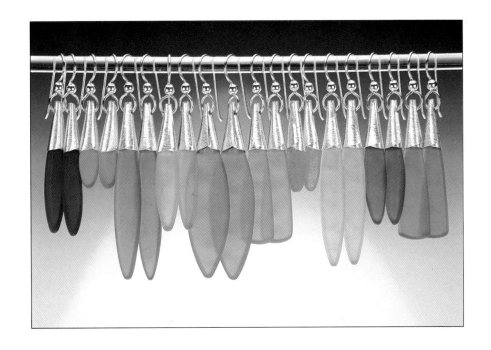

James Graham Photographer

Laura Pesce Glass

Of the many techniques incorporated into the jewelry of Laura Pesce, perhaps the most interesting and unusual is her revival of the art of making glass mosaics. This technique was first developed in ancient Rome and later refined by the Venetian glass masters of the 17th and 18th centuries. The jewelry that Pesce makes today combines in its design the ancient with the modern. The result is a synthesis of the ethnic and contemporary.

SHOWN: *Formelle*, earrings, mosaic glass and sterling, 2"L

Charles E. Medlin
M.H. Jackson Studios

Charles has received degrees from Western Carolina, Duke and Vanderbilt Universities. His designs include a wide range of mediums and processes, from traditional gold, silver and gold-plate work to the more cutting-edge mediums.

He is a member of the American Craft Council and the Society of Craft Designers, and has taken advanced coursework in jewelry at the Penland School of Crafts and the Gemological Institute of America.

SHOWN: Earrings and gold brooch

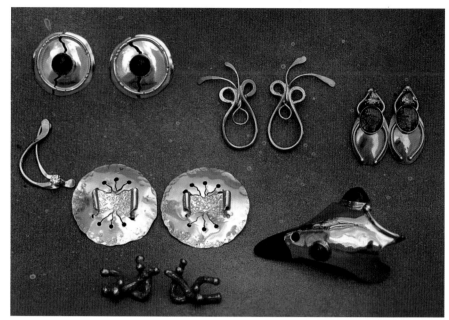

M.H. Jackson, York, SC

Barry Goodman and Son Jewelers

Barry incorporates sterling silver and 24K vermeil in 'botanical' style neckpieces, earrings, pins, bracelets and rings. His pieces achieve an earthly form with romantic lines. Barry, a 25-year veteran jeweler, has international recognition and regularly shows at the Buyers Market of American Crafts, Beckman's Handmade, and Handmade in USA shows.

Also see these GUILD publications: *Gallery Edition 1, 2; THE GUILD 1*

SHOWN: *Botanical Creations*, sampling of ten-flower collection, sterling and vermeil

Baird Metalwork Designs
David Baird

David has taken the idea of a bead to the very edge. Deformed, split, pieced, fractured, recombined and formed back into a unique wearable miniature sculpture. Produced in sterling silver and gold, embellished with gold, bronze and copper. Worn singly or in multiples, each bead is one-of-a-kind.

Sculptural earrings, brooches and bracelets in sterling silver, gold and copper by David push the boundaries of contemporary design.

Dean Powell

jmml designs
Jenny Levernier

Jenny has been making jewelry since 1981. Shown are one-of-a-kind sterling and stone pins, and bracelets. The sterling pieces take on a linear look, beautifully enhanced with stones.

Her mixed-metal earrings and pins focus on texture being created by piercing the metal, weaving wire, and stamping designs into the surface. She is also known for her production line of brass and nickel silver angels.

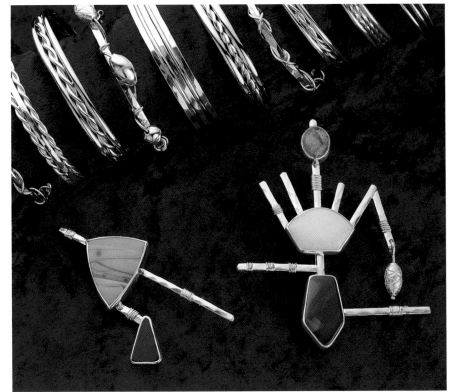

Wayne Torborg

Red Wolf Collection
Richard O'Brien

The Red Wolf Collection is authentically handcrafted American Indian style jewelry. Each piece in the collection is designed and crafted by Richard.

The Red Wolf Collection includes chokers, bracelets, belts and breastplates incorporating real bone and horn hairpipe, gemstones, and glass and metal beads, resulting in fine quality jewelry.

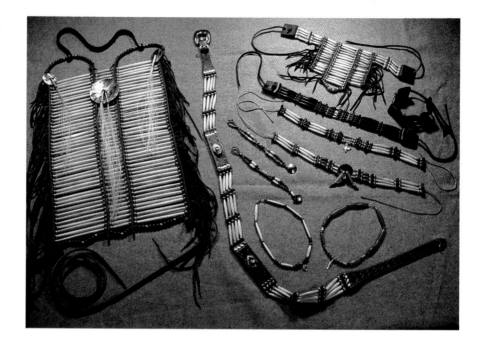

Kira J. Maer-lyn
Blessed Bead

Designer Kira J. Maer-lyn has been working with beads for over 20 years. She has created a *Gold 'n Glass* earring collection of gold-foiled blown and solid glass beads from Murano, Italy.

Kira is introducing her *Cascade Tie,* a one-of-a-kind piece to be worn by men as a stunning alternative to the bow tie. It is truly a breath-taking adornment for a man or a woman.

SHOWN: *Cascade Tie,* 1994, glass and semi-precious stone beads, 2 1/2" x 4"

Sergio Lub
Sergio Lub Handcrafted Jewelry, Inc.

Sergio creates contemporary renditions of classic and ethnic designs. A jeweler since 1969, Sergio has traveled through over 60 countries, learning the different techniques he uses in his jewelry, often reviving metal-working traditions and beliefs dating as far back as the Bronze Age.

His lifetime-guaranteed bracelets and rings are available in craft galleries and fine stores throughout the United States, Canada and Europe.

Ralph Gabriner

David Marson
Woodwear By David

David unites wood with Southwestern spirit to create a unique style of jewelry. Using multiple lamination techniques, both natural and dyed wood are formed into bracelets, earrings, pins and barrettes. Additional styles are enhanced by the use of sheet sterling silver with the wood laminations.

SHOWN: Bracelet, 3$^1/_2$" interior dimension, $^3/_4$"W x $^3/_{16}$" thick

Michele Alexander
Jewelry by Michele

'Fun to wear' is what comes to mind at first sight of Michele's jewelry. The mixed metals and assorted gemstones make it very versatile and collectable. It is unique in design, as well as affordable.

Each piece is handcrafted and a personal expression of jewelry as an art form.

SHOWN: *Mixed Metals Collection,* sterling, copper and gold-fill, accented with black onyx, blue lapis and amethyst

Jerry Anthony

Allen Bryan

Kristine Danielson

Kristine Danielson has always lived in the Great Lakes region of the United States, her favorite part being Michigan's Upper Peninsula. She is inspired by the beauty and wildness of these northern woods and waters.

Using a wide variety of technical skills, she combines copper, silver and gold, along with unique gems and minerals, to create and convey her ideas.

SHOWN: *Morning Dew,* great blue heron pin, sterling, copper, 14K and 22K gold, bi-color tourmaline, actinolited quartz, prehnite with copper

Gisela von Eicken
Gisela von Eicken Studio

How can we know the dancer from the dance?
W.B. Yeats

By weaving her Renaissance spirit into her definitive designs, Gisela von Eicken transforms the inanimate into animate … the physical into spiritual … and form into art.

Her 30-year body of work is Baroque in its detailing, yet modernistic in its design and chosen medium—fine gauge wire of every conceivable metal and color, often set with fossils, minerals and gems.

First exhibited at the Art Institute of Chicago, Gisela von Eicken's pieces can be seen internationally at museums and galleries.

SHOWN: *Pepperoni Pizza,* 1995, two pins, antique brass, sterling silver, garnet and crystal, each 2⁷/₈" × 3¹/₄" × 3¹/₈"

Kevin L. Goggin

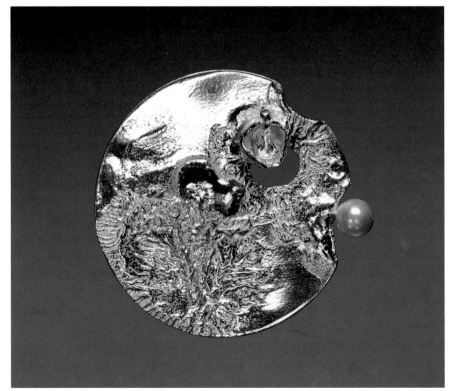

Brooch/pendant, 1995, fused sterling, fine, and reticulated silvers, 18K gold, cultured pearl, 2"Dia

John S. Cummings

Rita Rodgers
Deep Woods Designs

Rita Rodgers' jewelry reflects the textural quality of the landscapes of the mountainous region in which she lives. She creates her designs by fusing sterling, fine, and reticulated silvers with 18K gold accents. The designs may include pearls and/or gemstones. Because the design is created, in part, during fusion, each piece is distinct and unique.

Rita's handcrafted jewelry is designed for distinctness, wearability, and tactile appeal.

Marlena Genau

Ms. Genau is an artist metalsmith who exhibits her work at craft fairs and galleries across the country. Her work features the technique called 'anticlastic raising.' This is a hands-on process that stretches and compresses the metal into shape. Finished pieces have volume and depth; they are lightweight and strong.

SHOWN: *Knot Hoop* earrings, palladium and 18K gold (also available in silver and in 18K gold) 1³/₄" × 1³/₄" × ¹/₂"

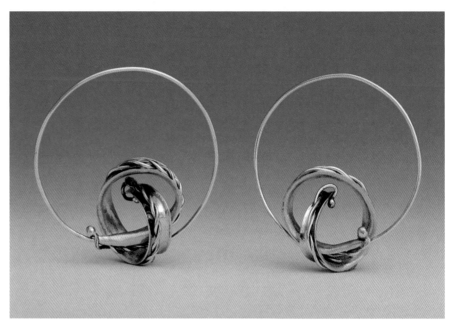

Scott McCue

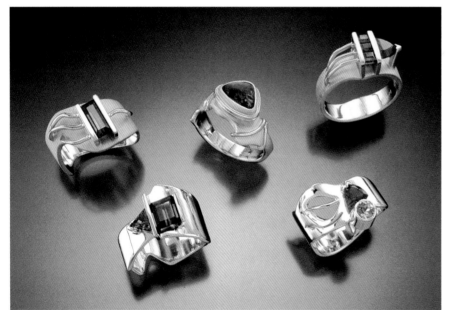

Ralph Gabriner

Vince Craft
Vince Craft Designs

Vince is best known for his contemporary bi-metal rings, innovatively designed with semi-precious gemstones that seem to float above unique sculpted bands.

Inspired by the Art Deco era and today's modern architecture, his work is asymmetrical and highly detailed, yet comfortable to wear.

Each piece is individually hand fabricated from 14K or 18K yellow gold and sterling silver sheet and wire, and accurately set with intensely colored gems resembling 'liquid fire.'

Debra Dembowski

The predominant focus of Debra Dembowski's jewelry is the nude. On a superficial level, Debra's work appears to be whimsical and sexually oriented. However, on a personal level, the choice of the figure in her work arises from a need to address interpersonal relationships.

Symbolism is an important aspect in her work. For instance, the elimination of certain features, such as the eyes or the mouth, within a particular earring couple or necklace may indicate limited vision or absence of communication. Debra enjoys playing with the elements of design to create work which can be interpreted on many different levels, ranging from eroticism to the celebration of the human form.

Debra has exhibited extensively at museums and galleries throughout the United States. Her work may also be purchased at the American Craft Council fairs.

Photos: Larry Sanders

Michael & Susan Overström

Overström Studio

"We design and make jewelry as the creative focus in our relationship, as well as the means to our individual growth and continued commitment to each other."
Michael and Susan Overström

The Overström Wedding Ring Collection, ©1995, is crafted by hand in sterling silver, 14K and 18K gold using techniques developed from 18 years of experience, dedication and commitment to the craft of fine jewelry making. Michael's Scandinavian heritage is evident in this collection of simple, clean ring designs.

Michael and Susan have been named finalists for the 1996 Niche Awards.

Pam Marraccini

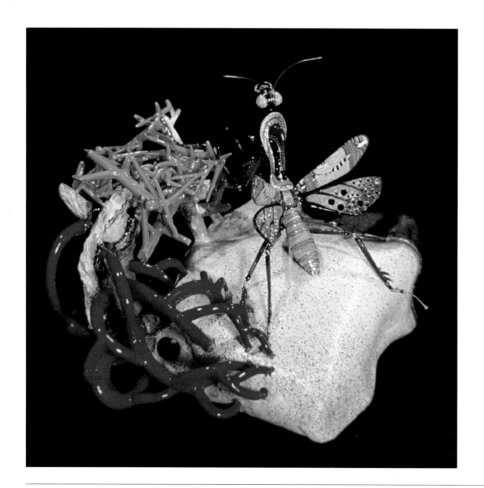

Cynthia Chuang
Erh-Ping Tsai

Jewelry 10, Inc.

Husband and wife team Cynthia Chuang and Erh-Ping Tsai have created a distinctive, unique line of three-dimensional porcelain jewelry and sculpture.

Their works of art capture the beauty and fascination of the natural world in imaginative interpretations, including 'creature' pins and one-of-a-kind pieces, that can be worn or displayed. They have earned recognition and many honors for their art.

SHOWN: *Preying Mantis*, wearable sculpture, porcelain, metal, and semi-precious beads, 5"H x 8"L x 5½"W

Deborah Sabo
Deborah Sabo Designs

Deborah finds inspiration in the ordinary occurances of everyday life. Through a wry sense of humor and extensive fine-art background, she transforms this into jewelry and accessories that are unique, yet convey a universal experience. Consequently, her handcrafted, reasonably priced artwork is sought after, with a growing collector base.

SHOWN: *She*, a jewelry stand with removable hand mirror displaying assorted pendants from the mask series, 24" x 9" x 7"

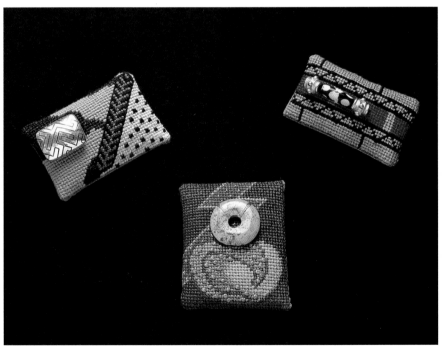

Ronald Matye

Susan Eileen Burnes

Susan Eileen Burnes creates needle-made fiber jewelry of fine wool, linen, silk and cotton. Each piece is made individually, completely stitched by hand, including hand-knotted cords on the necklaces.

Metallic threads and ornaments from around the world define and embellish each color-filled design.

These exuberant creations reflect Susan's admiration of all life-forms and encourage the wearer's imaginings. Completed brooches and necklaces are available and custom orders accepted.

CERAMICS CERAMICS

CERAMICS CERAMICS

Natalie Warrens
Natalie Warrens Ceramic Designs

Brightly airbrushed, underglazed earthenware pieces reflect Ms. Warrens' interest in movement, pattern and color. Her ability to wheel-throw very fine, thin plates, bowls and vessels gives her work an elegant glass-like quality rarely found in pottery. Although highly decorative, all work is functional and food safe.

Ms. Warrens' work is represented by more than 30 galleries throughout the United States and Canada.

Bowl, 1995, earthenware, 5"H x 14"Dia   Jim Piper

Laura Ross
Laura Ross/Contemporary Clay

Laura Ross's line of low-fired clay vessels reflects a commitment to fine craftsmanship and elegance of form. Richly colored air-brushed images are combined with etched lines, copper-leaf, and hand-dyed reeds to create a contemporary use of materials with traditional forms in clay. A wide range of sizes and color patterns is available.

Laura Ross's work is represented in galleries, museums shops and design centers throughout the United States.

Nancee Meeker

"If New York was a state that declared select artists and artisans 'Intangible Treasures,' potter Nancee Meeker would undoubtedly be one of them. Her work, as stunning as it is subtle, demands it."

Stuart Klein
Woodstock Times
August 11, 1994

Nancee Meeker, whose studio is in Rhinecliff, New York, has been a studio potter since 1973. Her stone-burnished and pit-fired vessels have been admired and collected by individuals, corporations and museums around the world—including the Smithsonian Institution in Washington and the Museum of Fine Arts, Boston.

After a sabbatical from clay—with travel and study in Ireland, Mexico, Turkey, Australia and New Zealand—Meeker's new works are more sensual in form, with complex patterns rising in subtle relief from the inside out. Her use of elaborate carving techniques, stone-burnished terra sigillatas, and hard-wood smoking, continues to give her pieces an exquisite look and feel. As with her previous work, they retain their organic, timeless elegance.

These vessels are decorative and are not meant to hold liquids.

SHOWN: *New Leaf* series, 1995, group of four, 8" to 14"H

Jeff Martin Studio, Eatontown, NJ

Susan M. Sipos
Object/Art

Exquisite, painterly pieces of striking beauty, with a remarkable color sense unmatched in current trends. Each piece conveys the attention and gesture of the hands that made it.

Susan M. Sipos holds B.F.A. and M.F.A. degrees from the Cleveland Institute of Art and the University of Illinois. Her works are in museums and collections worldwide. Creating works of intricate brilliance is her trademark of 25 years.

Microwavable and dishwasher safe.

Bridal registries welcomed.

"**metal** is durable and tough; I use a variety in my work. **Gold & Silver**, the *noble metals,* are distinguished by their *color,* as is the lesser metal **BRONZE**.

Recently, I started to work with ***pewter & palladium.*** They are wonderful metals: **silver-white** in color and very plastic."

Marlena Genau
Orinda, CA

Trent Tally

Terra Studios Inc.

Using elements of line, form, color and surface texture, Trent creates unique wheel-thrown vessels that are strongly influenced by primitive and ancient cultures. Each piece is individually raku fired, signed and dated.

Trent also produces architectural, high-fired stoneware, including large pots, murals, fountains and sculpture, for the enhancement of interior and exterior spaces.

A Lidded vessel with beaver, 1995,
   wheel thrown, raku fired, 13" x 11"

B Clay vessel, 1995, wheel thrown,
   raku fired, 11" x 11"

C Tall vessel, 1995, wheel thrown,
   raku fired, 14" x 8"

A

B

C

Jan Jacque

Jan Jacque captures her love of nature, trees, flora and quiet in her works of clay and wood. Her elegant, restful objects of art have matured over the past 20 years. The unique method of pit firing she has developed gives subtle depth and color to the organic forms. Another dimension of distinction comes from the incorporation of wood and mirrors in her clay creations. The long, complex process of combining wood and clay is testimony to the advanced skill and attention to detail that are important to this artist.

Custom work is welcomed. Additional photographs and information about the artist are available upon request.

A *Twilight Point*, 18"H x 12"W x 5"D

B *Moonlight Shadow*, 28"H x 16"W x 8"D

C *Sweeping Bough*, 32"H x 20"W

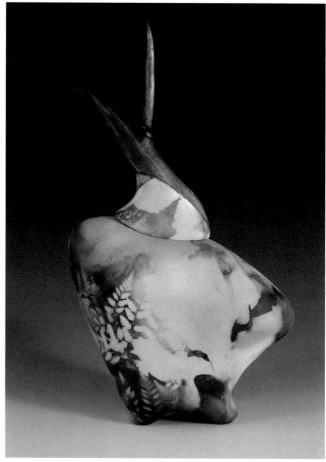

A

B

C

Chikako Ogata
JAPAN

Ms. Ogata lives and works in northern Kyushu, where the production of a variety of ceramic styles has flourished since the 17th century. Her hand-thrown porcelain ware is based on the style of the world-famous historical Imari ware. Ms. Ogata's training as a graphic designer and artist allow her to complement the refined shapes of her wares with spirited brushwork.

SHOWN: Blue-and-white porcelain bowl, 6"H x 13¾"Dia; compote and *sobachoko* cups

Norio Shikada

Lynn Duryea

Lynn Duryea has been working with terra cotta for over 20 years, exploring the relationship of color and form in her richly decorated and colorful work.

Lynn creates one-of-a-kind painted wall bowls and sculptural vessels, as well as functional plates, platters, bowls and planters. Lynn's work has been sold in galleries, shops and museum stores nationwide, and can be found in numerous public and private collections.

SHOWN: Untitled, hand-thrown terra cotta, slips and underglazes, oxidation fired, 16"Dia

Stretch Tuemmler

Betsy Ross
Betsy Ross Studio

Betsy Ross' work combines wheel thrown vessels with hand-built appendages. Her hand-painted earthenware is available in a multitude of finishes, from lustres to patinas.

Ms. Ross' new body of work features actual metallic patina surfaces (shown) representing a variety of metals. Her pieces evoke the sensation of finding some ancient artifact or treasure. She continues to offer the *Mini-Vessel* series, miniature renditions of her larger works, with the same attention to style and form.

Also see these GUILD publications: *Gallery Edition 1, 2; THE GUILD 5; Designer's Edition 6, 7, 8.*

"There are many reasons for art.
Some of the most compelling are ritual and function,
tied with purpose and meaning.

Our art tries to visually bring together feelings of time and space
gathered from our conscious and subconscious respect
for archeological tradition.

We envision figures fueled by imagination
and knowledge of past and present cultures,
and then try to create that environment."

Nancy and Allen Young
Albuquerque, NM

Carol Green Studio

Carol Green

A studio artist for over 20 years, Carol Green works in both clay and metal. Known primarily for her crystalline-glazed porcelain, in her most recent work she combines the raku process with fabricated copper and cast bronze.

Catalogs for raku vessels and crystalline-glazed porcelain available upon request.

SHOWN: *Jars*, mica impregnated clay, fabricated, patina copper lids, 13"H × 6"D and 8"H × 8"D

Boots Culbertson

Culbertson Pottery

Whimsi-cats, originally created for a special commission in 1980, are always evolving. Individually wheel thrown, sculpted and high-fired in several stoneware clays, they are known for catnapping, singing, showing off bead and macramé earrings, or just being sassy. Those shown are five to ten inches tall.

Other specialties from Culbertson Pottery include fountains, lamps, candelaria, functional ware and floor pieces.

Also see these GUILD publications: *Gallery Edition 1, 2; Designer's Edition 8*

Tom Dodson, Sarasota, FL

Bill FitzGibbons

Bill FitzGibbons is internationally known for his mixed-media artworks centering on comparative mythology. His work has been featured in major museums and in national and international art publications.

He has recently completed a series of raku ceramic masks. These pieces are created by a firing process that makes each ceramic piece unique. His *Shaman* series of masks evokes mystical feelings with engaging and powerful forms.

Please contact the artist about slides of available raku masks.

Richard Sargent

Catharine Hiersoux

Catharine Hiersoux's porcelain work explores sculpted vessel forms, augmented by vapor firings of wood and salt. Sizes range from 12" to 30" high.

Hiersoux has exhibited extensively and is represented in major collections, including the Renwick Gallery, Smithsonian Institution, Washington, DC; the Everson Museum, Syracuse, NY; the American Craft Museum, NY; the White House, Washington, DC.

The artist accepts commissions for both corporate and private work. Slides and additional information are available upon request.

SHOWN: *Rock Vessel: Chalice,* 12"H

Junko Yamada

JAPAN

Ms. Yamada has been engaged in pottery-making for over 20 years. She started her career by making clay sculptures and decorative objects, and is now interested in the creation of ceramic ware that has an earthy, yet decorative, quality. Her elegant ceramics, with touches of silver and gold, add a unique accent to any dinner table.

A Bowl, 3½" × 8½"Dia

B Cup and saucer, beer mugs

C Long plate, 15" × 4¾" × 2"

A

B

C

Photos: Kenichi Ogoshi

Jud Randall
Impressions in Clay

Jud Randall's *People Pots* represent the idea that we're all in this together regardless of social, economic or educational background, and that we all have a common bond.

Affectionately called 'Judlets,' the tiny body-language-expressive figures rely on the whole figure to show how they feel," says Randall.

SHOWN: *People Pots: We're All in This Together*, 1995, stoneware, 17"H

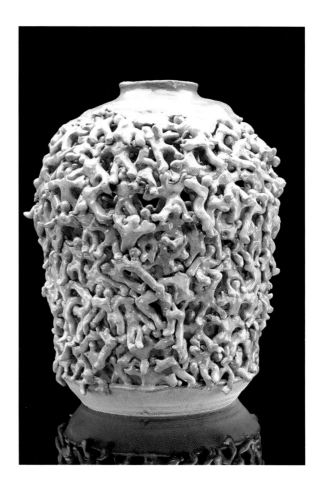

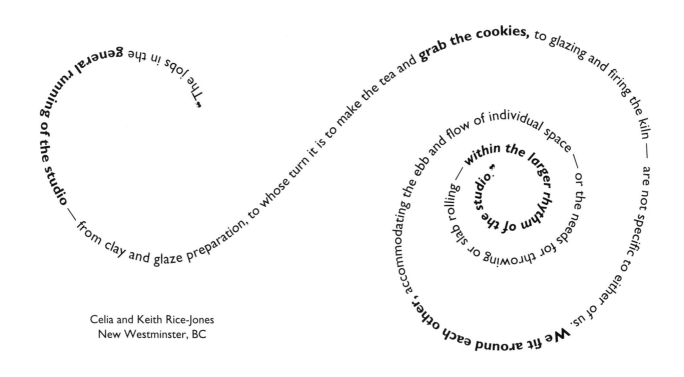

"The jobs in the general running of the studio — from clay and glaze preparation, to whose turn it is to make the tea and grab the cookies, to glazing and firing the kiln — are not specific to either of us, or the needs for throwing or slab rolling — accommodating the ebb and flow of individual space within the larger rhythm of the studio. We fit around each other,"

Celia and Keith Rice-Jones
New Westminster, BC

Surving Studios
Natalie and Richard Surving

Nature lovers from around the world covet Surving Studios' architectural ceramics.

The Surving's work has been exhibited in galleries and museums throughout the U.S. since the early 1970s. Surving's *Nature Tiles* are widely popular and readily available, both framed and for installation indoors or outdoors.

Natalie's unique sculptures are available on a limited basis. Major murals combining the sculpture and tile are Surving's favorite assignments.

SHOWN: From the *Water World Tile Series*, 6" × 6"

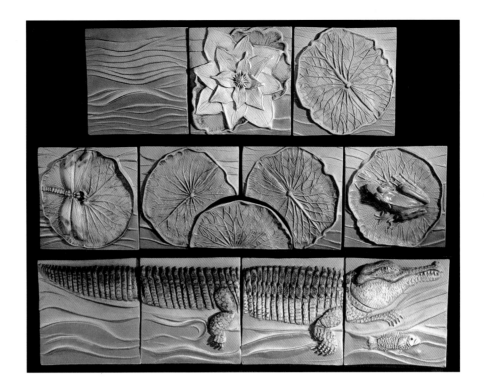

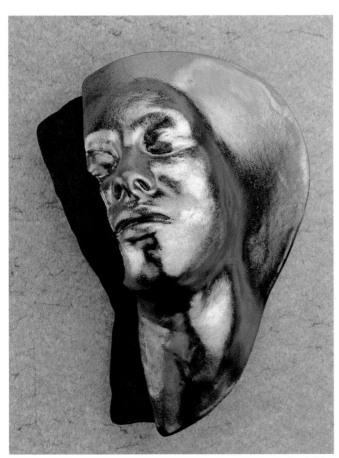

Hervé Grison

Dominique Blanchard
Dominique/Clayworks

Dominique is an artist from France who imbues his ceramic masks with a luminous spiritual energy. Archetypal themes of transformation from shadows to light, dreams, reflection, rebirth, enlightenment, inner peace and spiritual warriors are magically captured in these powerful sculptures.

Masterful blending of rich oxidation and reduction glazes with intricate textures is intensified by raku and low-fire techniques.

Information on additional shapes and styles is available upon request.

SHOWN: *Inner Peace*, raku fired, 12"H × 9"W

Dancing Fire Studio
Ann Lynn Whiteside

Works in clay by Ann Lynn Whiteside have evolved into large vessels, 18" to 27" high, with sensuous curves and wild patterns from nature.

Combining design, color theory and abstract patterning, she expresses both her concern for her fellow creatures and her own drive to create.

Each one-of-a-kind vessel is unique in shape and painted design.

Veldt Fur, Reptile and *Butterfly* in their natural habitat

Craig Tanner

Oval vases, 1995, stoneware, each approximately 10" x 2" x 12"

Robert Gray

David Changar Ceramic Designs
David Changar

David approaches ceramics as a designer first, trying to create forms that are modern and yet classic in line. The forms are hand thrown on the wheel, using either a black stoneware or a translucent grolleg porcelain. The work is glaze fired, in bright vivid colors, to vitrification, making it durable and non-porous.

David's designs are as varied as his glaze pallette. Work is available from tableware to sculptural forms.

Leroy Wheeler Parker

Multi-media artist Leroy W. Parker is very productive. He creates hundreds of large watercolors, ceramic vases and columns, permanent installations in concrete and ceramic, large colorful handmade paper pieces (8' × 4' and larger), and marbleized fabrics.

The vases shown here are examples of Mr. Parker's new work in clay. He has adapted imagery developed for his well-known paintings to the contour of these striking mid-sized (14" to 24") vessels. The pieces are hand-thrown, decorated with a translucent underglaze and clear overglaze, and raku fired.

Mr. Parker's work is included in many municipal and corporate collections throughout North America.

Please call for additional information.

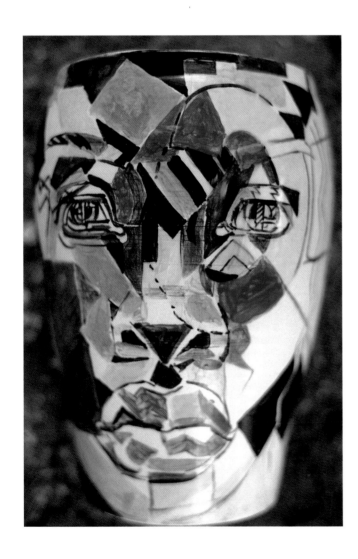
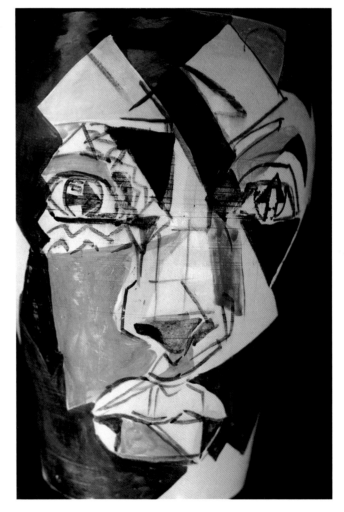

GLOSSARY OF CERAMIC TERMS

BISQUE PRELIMINARY FIRING TO HARDEN THE WARE FOR GLAZING.

BURNISHING DRY POLISHING OF A HARDENED, UNFIRED PIECE TO PRODUCE A GLAZE-LIKE SURFACE WHICH MAY BE FIRED.

CASTING A METHOD OF REPRODUCING IN QUANTITY BY USING LIQUID CLAY AND MOLDS.

CELADON GLAZE A GRAY-GREEN SEMI-OPAQUE TO OPAQUE GLAZE (REDUCTION FIRED).

A crystalline jar with sterling silver lid and malachite finial, by artist Carol Green, photo by Jerry Anthony

CHINA PAINT A LOW-FIRE GLAZE DECORATION APPLIED TO ALREADY GLAZED AND FIRED WHITEWARE OR PORCELAIN.

CLAY BODY A COMPOSITION OF VARIOUS CERAMIC MATERIALS.

COILING BUILDING THE WALLS OF POTTERY WITH ROPE-LIKE ROLLS OF CLAY, THEN SMOOTHING THE JOINTS.

CONE A SMALL, THIN PYRAMID OF CERAMIC MATERIAL MADE TO BEND AND MELT AT PRESCRIBED TEMPERATURES, PROVIDING A VISUAL INDICATION OF TEMPERATURE IN THE KILN.

CRACKLE GLAZE A GLAZE FEATURING MINUTE, DECORATIVE SURFACE CRACKS, SOMETIMES ACCENTED BY RUBBING WITH COLOR.

CRYSTAL(LINE) GLAZE A GLAZE FEATURING CLUSTERS OF CRYSTAL-LIKE SHAPES OR COLORS WITHIN A MORE UNIFORM, OPAQUE SURFACE.

EARTHENWARE TAN OR REDDISH POTTERY FIRED AT A LOW TEMPERATURE. IN AN UNGLAZED FORM, ITS POROSITY PREVENTS IT FROM HOLDING LIQUIDS.

FLAMEWARE A FLAMEPROOF WARE, AS DISTINCT FROM OVENWARE.

GLAZE THE GLASSY SURFACE COATING OF POTTERY. MANY VARIETIES ARE AVAILABLE.

HAND BUILT ASSEMBLED BY HAND. FINISHED OBJECTS MAY INCLUDE WHEEL-THROWN, CAST, COILED AND/OR SLAB ELEMENTS.

INLAY A DECORATING TECHNIQUE IN WHICH THE OBJECT IS INCISED WITH A DESIGN, A COLORED CLAY IS PRESSED INTO THE INCISIONS, AND THE SURFACE IS THEN SCRAPED TO CONFINE THE COLORED INLAY TO THE INCISIONS.

LOW FIRED CLAY FIRED AT A TEMPERATURE SUFFICIENT TO FUSE IT INTO A SOLID MASS, BUT TOO LOW TO MAKE IT COMPLETELY NON ABSORBENT.

LOW-FIRE GLAZES LOW-TEMPERATURE FINISHES, USUALLY ASSOCIATED WITH BRIGHT AND SHINY COLORS.

Charles Pearson and Timothy Roeder collaborated on this thrown and slab-built raku vessel

LUSTER A METALLIC OR IRIDESCENT EFFECT RESULTING FROM THE APPLICATION OF A THIN FILM OF METALLIC OXIDE.

MAT(TE) GLAZE A NON-GLOSS OR DULL-SURFACE GLAZE.

OXIDATION (OR OXIDATION FIRED) FIRING CERAMIC WARE AT HIGH TEMPERATURES AND WITHOUT REDUCING THE OXYGEN LEVELS IN THE ATMOSPHERE OF THE KILN. IT RESULTS IN LIGHTER, BRIGHTER COLORATIONS OF GLAZES.

GLOSSARY OF CERAMIC TERMS

PORCELAIN A HARDY CLAY BODY WHICH IS GLASSEOUS, WHITE AND SOMETIMES TRANSLUCENT.

RAKU POROUS EARTHENWARE ORIGINALLY MADE IN JAPAN AND ASSOCIATED WITH THE TEA CEREMONY. IT OFTEN HAS A SCORCHED LOOK, RESULTING FROM RAPID COOLING IN COMBUSTIBLE MATERIALS.

RAM PRESSED CLAY PRESSED INTO A MOLD BY A MACHINE, ALLOWING MULTIPLE REPRODUCTIONS OF THE SAME DESIGN.

REDUCTION (OR REDUCTION FIRED) FIRING CERAMIC WARE AT HIGH TEMPERATURES AND IN THE PRESENCE OF ADDED CARBON TO REDUCE THE PERCENTAGE OF OXYGEN IN THE KILN. THIS PRODUCES MUTED AND SUBTLE COLOR VARIATIONS.

SAGGAR A CLAY BOX IN WHICH POTTERY IS FIRED TO PROTECT THE WARE FROM FLAME AND ASH.

SALT GLAZE A HARD, GLASSY GLAZE RESULTING FROM THE VAPORS CREATED BY THE INTRODUCTION OF SALT INTO THE HOT KILN ATMOSPHERE. IT FREQUENTLY RESULTS IN AN ORANGE-PEEL TEXTURE.

SAWDUST-FIRED A PRIMITIVE FIRING TECHNIQUE IN WHICH SLOW-BURNING SAWDUST PRODUCES SUBTLE GRADATIONS OF COLOR.

SLAB BUILT CERAMIC WARE FORMED FROM FLAT PIECES OR 'SLABS.

SLIP CASTING PRODUCING OBJECTS USING PLASTER MOLDS AND LIQUID CLAY (SLIP). THIS METHOD ALLOWS FOR MULTIPLE REPRODUCTIONS OF THE SAME DESIGN.

SLIP GLAZES WATERY CLAY USED FOR DECORATIVE EFFECTS AND APPLIED BY POURING, DIPPING, BRUSH AND SPRAY.

STAIN ANY OXIDE OR PREPARED PIGMENT USED FOR COLORING BODIES, SLIPS OR GLAZES.

STONEWARE NATURAL CLAY, OR BLEND OF CLAYS, FIRED OVER 2100 DEGREES FAHRENHEIT FOR LITTLE OR NO ABSORBENCY. IT DIFFERS FROM PORCELAIN PRINCIPALLY IN COLOR, BEING GRAY, TAN OR REDDISH.

TERRA COTTA HARD, UNGLAZED, BROWN-RED EARTHENWARE CLAY, MOST OFTEN USED FOR CERAMIC SCULPTURE, INCLUDING SMALL FIGURES AND ARCHITECTURAL ORNAMENTS.

UNDERGLAZE PIGMENTS APPLIED TO THE RAW CLAY OR BISQUE AND COVERED WITH A TRANSPARENT GLAZE.

WAX RESIST DECORATION BY APPLYING WARM WAX TO POTTERY OR A LAYER OF GLAZE SO THAT A SUCCESSIVE LAYER OF GLAZE WILL NOT ADHERE TO THE WAX-DECORATED AREA.

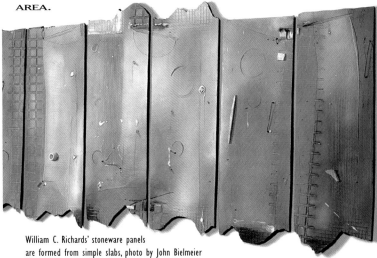

William C. Richards' stoneware panels are formed from simple slabs, photo by John Bielmeier

WHEEL THROWN FORMING OF POTTERY BY THE ACTION OF THE POTTER'S FINGERS AND HANDS AGAINST CLAY CENTERED ON THE REVOLVING PLATFORM OF A POTTER'S WHEEL.

WHITEWARE GENERIC TERM FOR WHITE CLAY BODIES USUALLY HIGH IN KAOLIN.

GLASS GLASS GLASS

GLASS GLASS GLASS

David New-Small

**New-Small & Sterling
Studio Glass, Ltd.**

David New-Small has been making glass since 1978. The *Marine Reliquary* series is a result of his experiences and concern with the marine environment that he explores as a scuba diver. The reliquary contains in its walls the memories of the sea seen for the first time in this century.

David New-Small's work is in collections around the world, including the Corning Museum.

SHOWN: *Marine Reliquary—ARV256*, 1994, blown glass, 23 cm (9")Dia

Kenji Nagai

Michele Savelle

Michele's bowls tell stories, each one unique, with imagery derived from many experiences and sources. Most have a humorous angle.

All are fused and slumped glass, with an area of handmade glass in the center of the bottom of each one.

Michele studied at Pilchuck Glass School, shows nationally, and teaches in the Seattle area.

Also see the *Gallery Edition 1, 2.*

SHOWN: *Earth, Angel and Singing Dog,* 16"W x 8"H

Andiamo Glass Design

Robert Spielholz
& Kathleen Hargrave

Robert Spielholz and Kathleen Hargrave are
nationally recognized glass artists from the
Pacific Northwest. Robert has been blowing
glass for 25 years. Kathleen, originally a print-
maker, joined Robert to found Andiamo
Glass Design in 1986.

Robert and Kathleen collaborate to produce
vessels and other forms with colorful, playful
and often narrative imagery. They employ
a variety of techniques, including surface
etching, traditional graal, and enameled and
cased glass.

See the studio's homepage at:
http://www.artglass.com/andiamo/

A *Arabesque*, 1995, blown glass, etched,
 painted and cased, 16"H x 9"W

B *Tulambin*, 1995, blown glass, etched,
 painted and cased, 12"H x 10"W

C *Angsoka*, 1995, blown glass, etched,
 painted and cased, 12"H x 11"W

A

B

C

Mesolini Glass Studio

Gregg Mesmer
Diane Bonciolini

Beauty, functionality and uniqueness are hallmarks of Gregg Mesmer and Diane Bonciolini's kiln-formed glass dishware. Befitting tables casual or formal, these dishes can be used and enjoyed. With little effort, your present dishware or china can be updated or enhanced. Perfect for the sophisticated glass collector or a new bride, Mesolini dishware can create a lasting impression.

The cut-off edge is their distinctive signature. Each piece is signed, dated and numbered.

Susan Marie Anderson, Seattle, WA

California Glass Studio

Nina Paladino Caron
Michael K. Hansen

Michael and Nina have been working together for 18 years. Their glass is represented internationally in galleries and in private and corporate collections.

A complete catalog of other glass work is available. Send $3.00 for the 12-page, full-color brochure, refunded with first order.

SHOWN: *Water Lily*, free-form bowl, 21" to 24"Dia, signed and numbered, limited edition

Nourot Glass Studio

Michael Nourot, Ann Corcoran & David Lindsay

Collaborators Michael Nourot, Ann Corcoran and David Lindsay have been making all kinds of functional decorative works in glass since 1974. Glassmakers to the Pope, presidents, and major corporations, the studio is known for outstanding quality and value in vividly colored original designs. Each is signed and registered. Gift cards included. Catalog available; video, articles upon request. Dozens of styles in each: perfume bottles, paperweights, vases, bowls, platters.

A *Hunt Bowl* in red with gold
    satin luster glass interior,
    8"H × 9 1/2"D

B *Large Red Fluted Vase*,
    14"H × 12 1/2"W; 4 1/2" base

A

B

Photos: Paul Berg

Jeremy Lawrence Design

Jeremy Lawrence

Jeremy Lawrence has recently created a unique etching process for glass and wall mirrors. His designs are photographically applied to 'frost' images into the backs of mirrors for a permanent and elegant look.

Mr. Lawrence has created custom-etched glass furniture for private and corporate collections in New York City since 1985.

Catalog available of many styles to match interior designs.

SHOWN: *Romance*, 1994, etched, beveled mirror, 22" × 28"

Absolute Images

Markroy Studio

Mark Bleshenski

Rich in depth, cast glass panels can be used as elements in table tops, lighting and architectural settings, as well as purely decorative stand-alone objects.

Their extraordinary capacity to capture light contributes to the ambiance of any interior, making them an ideal focal point in bright or dim environments.

Textured panels and custom designs of almost any shape can be made. Sizes to about 2' × 3' can be tiled for larger applications.

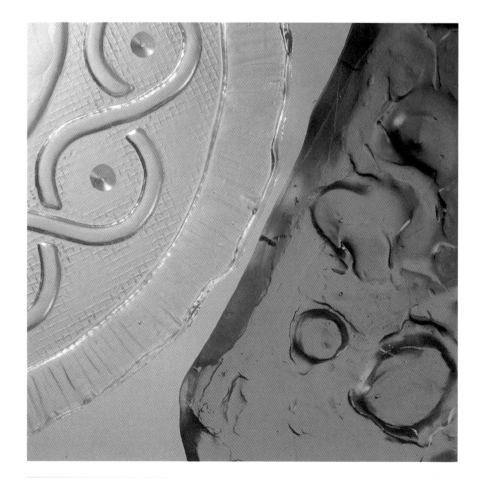

Larry Zgoda

Larry Zgoda Studio

Larry Zgoda's series of stained glass sculptures are titled *Architonomous Art Glass.* Drawing inspiration from architecture, Larry Zgoda created the *Architonomous* format as a way of presenting his original designs in a gallery setting. Requiring neither hanging nor installation, these works are suitable for placement on desk, table, credenza or window ledge.

Architonomous is an amalgam of the words 'architecture' and 'autonomous.' Zgoda, who has spent over 20 years working in architectural stained glass, offers these sculptures in editions, as well as singular works.

Photos: Richard Bruck

Hulet Glass
Dinah Hulet

Dinah Hulet uses primarily soft glass, imported from Italy, to create one-of-a-kind marbles. She achieves precise detail of color and design by delicate manipulation of the surface of molten glass. Incorporating a variety of lampworking techniques, including original portrait, picture, and mosaic cane murrini, she creates small works of art.

SHOWN: Marbles, approximately ⁷/₈", 1" and 1¹/₂", each signed and dated

"IT IS ALWAYS
TERRIBLY IMPORTANT TO ME
THAT EVERYONE KNOW THAT THEIR INVOLVEMENT
WITH THE SEEN AND THE UNSEEN WORLD
IS DIRECTLY RELATED TO THEIR WELL-BEING,
A WAY OF 'FALLING INTO' LIFE AND LIFE'S FORCES
THAT MAKES ONE BECOME ONESELF
AND BY SUCH KNOWLEDGE,
RESPONSIBLE FOR OURSELVES, OUR EARTH,
OUR PEOPLE, OUR UNIVERSE.
SUCH MESSAGES ARE EMBODIED IN ALL MY WORK."

TONI PUTNAM
GARRISON, NY

California Glass Studio

Nina Paladino Caron
Michael K. Hansen

Michael and Nina have been working together for 18 years. Their glass is represented internationally in galleries and in private and corporate collections.

Pictured are hand-blown glass perfume bottles paperweights using dichroic glass .

A complete catalog of other glass work is available. Send $3.00 for the 12-page, full-color brochure, refunded with first order.

A Dichroic perfume bottles, teal, cobalt, amethyst and black

B Dichroic paperweights, cobalt, teal, amethyst and black

A

B

Slumped and fused tableware from Mesolini Glass Studio, photo: Susan Marie Anderson, Seattle, WA

BATCH A QUANTITY OF RAW MATERIALS MIXED IN PROPER PROPORTIONS AND PREPARED FOR FUSION IN A GLASS FURNACE.

CAMEO/INTAGLIO A TECHNIQUE IN WHICH THE FINISHED GLASS FORM IS COVERED WITH ANOTHER COATING OF GLASS OF A DIFFERENT COLOR INTO WHICH IS CARVED OR ETCHED A DESIGN WHICH EXPOSES THE BASE COLOR.

CASED GLASS GLASS COMPLETELY COVERED (THROUGH BLOWING OR DIPPING) BY OTHER, USUALLY DIFFERENTLY COLORED, GLASS. OUTER LAYERS CAN BE PARTIALLY CUT AWAY TO REVEAL COLOR(S) OF THE PREVIOUS 'CASTINGS' BENEATH.

COPPER FOIL TECHNIQUE JOINING GLASS BY APPLYING ADHESIVE COPPER TAPE TO EACH PIECE AND SOLDERING THE COPPER TOGETHER.

ENAMELED GLASS DECORATED WITH PARTICLES OF TRANSLUCENT — USUALLY COLORED — GLASS OR GLASS-LIKE MATERIAL, WHICH FUSES TO THE SURFACE UNDER HEAT. MULTI-COLORED DESIGNS, AS WELL AS MONOCHROME COATINGS, CAN BE CREATED.

ETCHED GLASS GLASS DECORATED OR OTHERWISE MARKED BY THE USE OF HYDROFLUORIC ACID. THE GLASS IS FIRST COVERED WITH AN ACID-RESISTANT WAX OR GUM, THE DESIGN IS DRAWN THROUGH THE RESIST WITH A POINT, AND THE EXPOSED GLASS IS ETCHED BY THE ACID.

Stephan J. Cox's perfume bottles are carved with a diamond saw, then sand-blasted, photo: Don Pitlik, Minneapolis, MN

GLOSSARY OF GLASS TERMS

FREE BLOWN (FREEHAND BLOWN) GLASSWARE SHAPED BY AIR PRESSURE, SUCH AS MOUTH-BLOWING THROUGH A METAL TUBE ('PIPE') TO WHICH MOLTEN GLASS ADHERES.

Etched ginger vase by Michael K. Hansen and Nina Paladino Caron, photo: Tommy Olaf Elder

FUMED GLASS GLASS WITH AN IRIDESCENT SURFACE.

GRAAL TECHNIQUE GLASS WHICH IS 'BLOWN TWICE.' THE GLASS IS MADE WITH A COLOR OVERLAY WHICH IS THEN CUT, ETCHED OR SANDBLASTED WITH A DECORATION. THE PIECE IS SUBJECTED AGAIN TO THE HEAT OF THE FURNACE TO IMPART FLUIDITY AND SMOOTHNESS TO THE DESIGN, AND THEN ENCASED IN LEAD CRYSTAL.

HOT GLASS GLASS WORKED IN ITS MOLTEN STATE DIRECTLY FROM THE FURNACE, USUALLY IN THREE DIMENSIONS. THE TERM IS USED IN CONTRAST TO 'STAINED GLASS,' WHICH IS USUALLY FLAT-WORKED COLD.

LAMP WORK THE TECHNIQUE OF MANIPULATING GLASS BY HEATING IT WITH A SMALL FLAME.

LEADED GLASS GLASS CONTAINING A PERCENTAGE OF LEAD OXIDE, WHICH INCREASES ITS DENSITY AND IMPROVES ITS ABILITY TO REFRACT AND DISPERSE LIGHT. IT IS USED FOR ORNAMENTS AND FOR DECORATIVE AND LUXURY TABLEWARE.

OFF-HAND BLOWN GLASS GLASS WHICH IS SHAPED AND FINISHED BY BLOWING AND WITH HAND TOOLS RATHER THAN BY USING MOLDS.

SAND-BLASTED GLASS GLASS WHOSE SURFACE IS BLOWN WITH FINE SAND UNDER HIGH PRESSURE. IT RESULTS IN A ROUGHENED, NON-TRANSPARENT SURFACE (OFTEN CALLED 'FROSTED'). DEEPLY ENGRAVEED PATTERNS CAN ALSO BE PRODUCED BY USING PROTECTIVE STENCILS.

SLUMPED GLASS PRECAST GLASS, SUCH AS PLATE GLASS, WHICH IS HEAT-SOFTENED AND MOLDED OVER FORMS.

SODA-LIME CRYSTAL A TYPE OF GLASS NOT PARTICULARLY RESISTANT TO HEAT AND USED IN WINDOWS AND BOTTLES.

SURFACE DECORATION MANY CHEMICAL AND PHYSICAL SUBSTANCES ARE APPLIED TO HOT GLASS DURING THE BLOWING PROCESS, OFTEN BY ROLLING THE HOT GLASS OVER A TABLE ON WHICH A SUBSTANCE HAS BEEN SPRINKLED. COMMONLY USED ARE POWDERED OR CRUSHED GLASS AND SILVER NITRATE.

Jonathan Winfisley uses cased glass to create these fluid forms for his Madonna Series ©1995

METAL METAL METAI

METAL METAL METAL

Baird Metalwork Designs
David Baird

Chaos Series.
Functional Sculpture.
Metal and Glass.

Inspired by the chaotic structure of a wind-blown field of grass, reduced to a sculptural form surrounding glass, David creates one-of-a-kind sculptures from metal and glass.

SHOWN: Bowl, silverplated brass wire and glass, 3" x 10" x 10"

Dean Powell

Fred Danforth
Danforth Pewterers

Fred Danforth, a descendant of renowned pewtersmiths dating back to colonial times, has revitalized the Danforth tradition of excellence in exquisite hand-spun pewter heirlooms. Each piece is individually hand-crafted from the finest pewter alloy. Elegant and classic oil lamps, vases, candlesticks and bowls are a few of the designs in this line of signed original and functional pieces.

Onion Oil Lamp (left) and *Mariner Oil Lamp*, winner of the 1994 American Pewter Guild Design Award

Enhancements

Deborah Jemmott

Deborah Jemmott designs and produces classically contemporary tableware and accessory pieces. Her powerful linear designs are finely crafted in a variety of metals.

Deb believes that people's lives are enhanced by living with art—and that art which can be used is easy to live with. Thus, she views the functional art she creates as *Enhancements*. These include tableware, candle stands, vases, office accessories, custom sculptures, lighting and small tables.

Her work can be seen in many shops and galleries across the country and numerous custom pieces are in private collections.

A *Spiral Salad Tongs* and *Spiral Hors d'oeuvre Forks*, sterling or nickel

B *Demitasse Spoons* and *Small Spreader Knife with Garnet*, sterling or nickel

C *ZigZag Salad Servers*, palladium plate over nickel or sterling

A

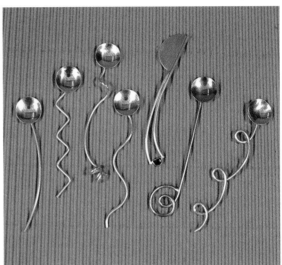

B

C

Tom Torrens Sculpture Design

Using strong, simple forms and familiar materials, Tom Torrens fashions works of uncommon strength and character. For the past 20 years, Mr. Torrens has designed and produced high-quality, functional works of art from recycled and industrial materials.

Mr. Torrens received his M.F.A. degree in sculpture from Washington University at St. Louis, and taught sculpture at the university level for 15 years. Mr. Torrens maintains a full-time design studio in Washington state, where he lives with his wife and son.

Functional sculptures from the Torrens collection include fountains, bells, gongs, birdfeeders, birdbaths, indoor and outdoor lighting, tables, candleholders and gates. Commissioned works are also available. Materials used are Cor-ten and mild steel, copper, cedar and stainless steel.

Free catalog available.

Also see these GUILD publications:
THE GUILD 1; Architect's Edition 11.

James J. Durant Enterprises

James J. Durant

For over 30 years, James Durant has hand-crafted solid brass aviaries the same way … perfectly.

Perfection doesn't come easy. Beginning with the finest solid brass and copper, each aviary is handcrafted, assembled and polished, until the demands of perfection are carefully satisfied.

Each aviary is more than a beautiful creation … it's a functional birdcage. Various cage sizes, wire gauges and spacings are available to accommodate birds of every size, from finches to macaws. Custom commissions are accepted. Crated for domestic and international shipment.

Birds and Beasts

Dave Johnson

Dave has created an assortment of whimsical creatures and other metal sculptures from discarded farm implements and tools. Each piece is unique and has its own personality.

They can be found ornamenting homes, gardens, and public displays across the country.

A *Springer*, 1994, 6' × 4'

B *Duke*, 1995, 2' × 3'

Roux Roux
Steve and Anita Vaubel

Steve and Anita Vaubel, jewelry designers, have created Roux Roux, a line of products including drawer pulls, corkscrews, bottle stoppers, coat racks, mirror frames, lamps and metal containers. All figures have threaded brass sleeves for a secure fit.

Figures are offered in a variety of sizes with 80 different designs available. Will create custom work based on client's theme.

Catalog available.

ARK NY Inc.
Amy Hess and Ed Batcheller

Amy Hess and Ed Batcheller operate a little organization in New York called ARK NY Inc.

They design and produce fanciful objects, made of nickel-plated steel, for the home. Many are based on animal themes such as horses, dogs, fish and other creatures.

All items are handcrafted and signed by the artist.

Judie Bomberger

Over the past five years, internationally recognized artist Judie Bomberger has been bringing to life the whimsical figures born in her imagination, and consequently making people smile!

Using a whimsical theme throughout, Judie creates art for both the home and garden.

Her work ranges from hand-cut metal sculpture, both painted and rusted, to whimsical watercolor prints and hand-wrought and painted candleholders.

The colorful characters found in Judie's watercolor prints often serve as inspiration for her metal sculpture.

A *Starman*, two-dimensional painted metal sculpture, approximately 19"H

B *Adopting Oreo*, print-inspired painted metal sculpture, approximately 24"H

C Vessels, hand-wrought and painted steel, approximately 12"H

A

B

C

Photos: George Post

Toni Putnam

This Pyrrhic Sphinx is a maquette for a life-size bronze of the same name. With her broken and missing parts, she evokes the grievous losses experienced by the king of Epirus in his victories over the Romans at Heraclea and Asculum (279-280 AD).

The sphinx is very ancient. Her time has passed. We do not understand her anymore.

SHOWN: *Pyrrhic Sphinx Recumbent*, bronze with gold leaf, 13" × 13"

Ted Spiegel

"My interest in weaving was first sparked after seeing it demonstrated on ABC's 'Good Morning America.' Several days later, a co-worker told me about looms for sale, and I was soon the proud owner of two looms, various tools and supplies. That's how it all started. Since I had no knowledge of the art, the retiring weaver whose tools I'd purchased passed on his knowledge and expertise in exchange for fishing privileges on my pond."

Rose Marie Patrick
Rainbow Rugs by Rose
Hop Bottom, PA

Metalweavings

Suzanne Donazetti
Kenneth Payne

Suzanne Donazetti and Kenneth Payne create contemporary abstract images in metal. They translate the art of tapestry weaving into a colorful medium of gilded, painted and molded copper.

Elegant frames/mirrors, clocks, blank books, boxes, coiled baskets, tables, and wall sculptures are handcrafted using a unique process of coloring copper. Each original, signed piece is durable and easily maintained.

Metalweavings are represented in more than 100 craft galleries, as well as corporate and private collections.

A Grouping of mirror, clocks, and small coiled basket; mirror: 12½"H

B Frame/mirror, 8"H × 8"W

C Clock, 14"H

D Basket, traditional coiling and twining techniques, 3"H × 8"Dia

A

B

C

D

GLOSSARY OF METAL TERMS

Betsy King's pins are constructed from sterling silver, copper, paper and plexiglass, photo: Tom Hodge

BASE METAL
Any metal other than a precious metal, such as copper or zinc.

CASTING
The process of pouring molten metal into a hollow mold. The cast metal duplicates the object (wood, hard wax, etc.) originally impressed in the mold material. Some processes permit more than one reproduction.

CHASED
Metal with a surface patterned by striking with a hammer or other non-cutting tool. Applied to one surface of the metal only, this process is often combined with repoussé to achieve greater detail.

CLOISSONÉ
Enameling in which the colors are separated by thin metal ribbons or wires to maintain the pattern and keep the melting colors from running together.

CONTRUCTED
(1) Hand made in parts and assembled to form a whole. (2) Not cast.

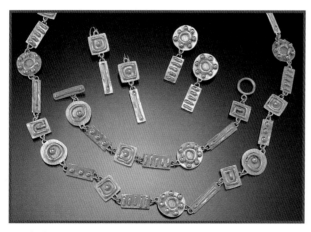

Jewelry by Barbara A. Hirschfeld, made with a combination of casting and hand-fabricating techniques, photo: Ralph Gabriner

ELECTROFORMED
Creation of a metal object by electrically depositing metal on a master form of wax. After the wax is removed, a metal shell remains.

ELECTROPLATED
Coated with a thin layer of (usually precious) metal by passing an electric current through a chemical solution containing a source of the metal.

FABRICATED
An object made in parts and assembled to form a whole.

FORGED
Metal shaped, usually by hammering, while at a red or white heat in blacksmithing, but usually cold in jewelry.

GRANULATION
Tiny balls of metal heat-fused to a metal surface without the use of solder.

HOLLOWWARE
Vessels, such as bowls and pitchers.

Jayne Redman used a combination of raising and repoussé to create this small scent bottle, photo: Jim Daniels

LOST WAX CASTING
A one-time reproduction process in which an object (as of wax) is impressed into sand or surrounded with a special plaster to make a mold. The wax is burned out, and molten metal takes the form of the 'lost' wax.

MARRIED METAL
Patterns or imagery developed by joining various colored alloys, such as of bronze, copper and silver, adjacent to one another.

OXIDIZE
Natural darkening and coloring of metal when exposed to oxides in the air. Can be accelerated or controlled for effect.

GLOSSARY OF METAL TERMS

David M. Bowman's patinated, etched vase is made from brass sheet

PATINA (1) A surface coloring, usually brown or green, produced by oxidation of bronze or other metal. It occurs naturally or can be produced artificially for decorative effect. (2) The substance used to produce the effect. (3) A surface luster occurring from age or use.

RAISED Hammering a flat sheet of metal into a container-type form.

REPOUSSÉ ('REH-POO-SAY') A design raised in relief on a metal surface, or the process of hammering (on both sides) to achieve it.

RESIN A plastic which may be bonded to metal or cast in molds.

RETICULATED A metal surface delicately wrinkled by a special heating process.

SAND-CAST To produce a casting by pouring molten metal into sand molds.

WROUGHT Shaped by beating or hammering, often elaborately, for decorative effect. Wrought iron is also a low-carbon metal which can be elongated without breakage and is resistant to corrosion.

Hand-wrought steel candleholders from Judie Bomberger, photo: George Post

MIXED & OTHER MEDIA

MIXED & OTHER MEDIA

Elliot Landes
Penmakers

Elliot Landes has been producing handmade wood writing instruments and accessories for 20 years. His work is represented in 400 galleries in the United States and around the world. He makes fountain pens, rolling writers, pencils and boxes, like the one shown, that lift up the contents when one opens the lid. The pen clip is serpentine shaped and has a handmade wood ball that matches the wood of the pen.

Melodious
Lori Axelson

Melodious presents music, animation and function in irresistible combinations. From musical clocks to musical toy chests, our furniture and accessories are guaranteed to delight the child in every music box lover and the music box lover in every child.

The Melodious collection is hand painted with durable non-toxic acrylics in rich, original colors. Each piece is carefully constructed to provide lasting service and fun.

Catalog available.

Clockwise: musical treasure chest, musical mirror, musical picture frame, musical step stool, musical clock

Jon Bonjour

Judy Ditmer

Judy Ditmer has been turning wood full-time for nine years. Her beautifully detailed salad bowls have a food-safe finish and are a delight to use. These and her sculptural pieces are sold in galleries across the nation.

She has written two books on wood turning: *Basic Bowl Turning* and *Turned-Wood Jewelry*, both published by Schiffer Publishing, Ltd.

SHOWN: Salad bowl, 1995, lathe-turned box elder, 6¼"H x 12½"Dia

Russ's Rural Rockers

Russ Jacobsohn

Russ's Rural Rockers are individually crafted by hand from solid hardwoods such as walnut, cherry and mahogany.

Each horse has a hand-rubbed oil finish, a saddle of genuine leather, and a replaceable mane and tail of 100% cotton.

These horses are durable enough to gallop through the fantasies of many generations of delighted children.

Each handcrafted piece is signed and dated.

SHOWN: Mahogany rocker, 250 lb. weight limit, 40"L x 35"H x 16"W (also available 58"L x 45"H x 24"W)

John Lucas

Etsuko Kamijo

Kigi no Uta
JAPAN

Ms. Kamijo has been engaged in wood craft for more than 25 years. Her initial training was in the making of musical instruments. Total familiarity with her medium gives her an unrivaled confidence in the tinting and joining and carving of woods such as pine and cedar to create objects with a bold and elegant line.

SHOWN: Wooden shell plate, 12" x 8" x 4"H

Kunikatsu Seto

JAPAN

Mr. Seto lives and works in Wajima, on the Noto Peninsula, where the best Japanese *urushi* lacquerware is produced. His techniques are traditional, but his aesthetic expression is totally contemporary. Abstract applications of fabric under numerous layers of lacquer is his favored idiom.

SHOWN: *Nuno* bowl, zelkova base with fabric attached and lacquered, 5"H x 9¼"Dia

Robert B. Lash
Iron & Clay

Influenced by ancient forms and processes which give his work a timeless feel, Robert B. Lash creates suspended vessels which combine forged iron and clay.

Graceful forms within a frame create a striking balance of shape and volume. His work possesses mysterious and ageless qualities which evoke images of primitive rituals and ceremonies.

Works shown are from the *Vessels of Spirit* series.

A Forged iron and clay,
   15"H x 20"W x 6"D

B Forged iron,
   30"H x 16"W x 11"D

C Forged iron and raku-fired vessel,
   25"H x 15"W x 6"D

A

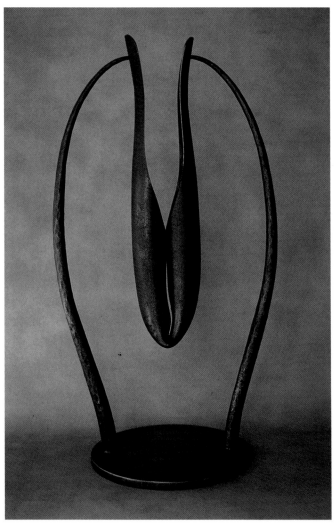

B

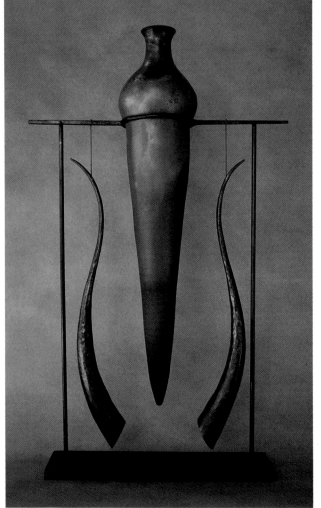

C

Cheryl Battaglia

Inspired by the classical, Cheryl Battaglia designs and constructs one-of-a-kind and limited-edition architectural boxes, some opening in as many as eight places. Boxes are painted and gilded in 23K gold.

Ms. Battaglia's boxes are in private collections throughout the United States and have been exhibited in the windows of Tiffany & Company.

The pieces, though functional, are frequently used as strictly decorative objects and enjoyed for their elegant simplicity and the feeling of tranquillity they evoke.

They are also used as special hideaways for personal treasures, cherished objects and collections.

A   One-opening monument with gold ball,
    $5\frac{1}{2}$" × $3\frac{1}{2}$" × $3\frac{1}{2}$"

B   One-opening monument, $4\frac{1}{2}$" × 4" × 4"

C   Three-opening monument with gold ball,
    7" × $2\frac{1}{2}$" × $2\frac{1}{2}$"

A

B

C   Architectural boxes by Cheryl Battaglia

The Philosopher's Stone

John Hannah & Tamar Drushka

John Hannah and Tamar Drushka work with the ancient glacial stones of Nova Scotia to create beautiful one-of-a-kind stone vessels. The inherent beauty of each stone is enhanced by the cutting and the hand-rubbed finish of natural oils. Their work is distinguished by its sensual textures and rich, lustrous surfaces.

These timeless pieces bring an atmosphere of calm to a hurried world. Pieces shown range in height from 2¹/₂" to 9".

Peter Barss, Bridgewater, Nova Scotia

J. Todd Barber

Intrigued with the history and applications of leather, Todd Barber has worked in this ancient medium for more than 25 years.

The primitive and contemporary techniques used in his leather art, coupled with its aroma, entice the viewers' senses and challenge their curiosity.

The hallmark of Barber's benchwork can be seen in the award-winning boxes he creates. Ornamental in nature, they incorporate the use of semi-precious stones and cultural artifacts. Each piece is one-of-a-kind.

SHOWN: *Textured Angles #2*, 1995, hand-tooled and dyed, pressure-laminated leather box with morrisonite jasper, 6¹/₂"H x 6¹/₂"L x 5"W

Juno Sky Studio
Betty Fulmer

An understanding of the interpretive possibilities of a variety of materials, along with two decades of technical innovation, has enabled the artist to create unique paperworks of rich color, sensual texture, and emotive content. Opulent and engaging, the works incorporate handmade paper, iridescent acrylics, gold leaf, wood, and brass wire. They are protection-treated for durability.

The artist's works are included in public and private collections in the U.S. and Europe. Recent commissions include the Marathon Oil Co., the Toledo Museum of Art, U.S. Gypsum, Hyatt Regency Hotels, the Thermos Corp., and the U.S. Customs Service.

Commissions and site-specific projects are welcome.

A *Spirit Vessels*, handmade paper, gold leaf, wood, acrylic, tallest vessel 24"H × 8"Dia, from the Juno Sky Precious Earth Collection

B *New Millennium*, handmade paper, gold leaf, acrylic, 46" × 66", from the Juno Sky Precious Earth Collection

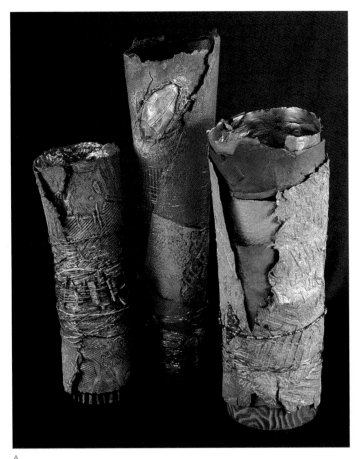

A

B

Photos: Douglas Cameron

Leroy Wheeler Parker

Art on Wheels

Multi-media artist Leroy W. Parker is very productive. He creates hundreds of large watercolors, ceramic vases and columns, permanent installations in concrete and ceramic, large colorful handmade paper pieces (8' x 4' and larger), and marbleized fabrics.

In addition, Mr. Parker is making very new inroads by printing manhole covers on his handmade paper. He plans to create manhole art from every metropolis and in many countries by making direct prints on site.

Mr. Parker's work is included in many municipal and corporate collections throughout North America.

Please call for additional information.

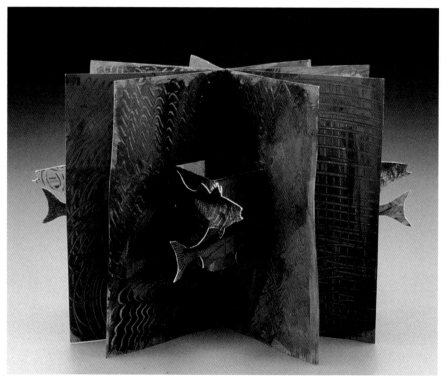

Fish Book II, 1994, spring-bound book, 8"W x 12"H when closed

Zolton Cohen

River Weaving and Batik Company

Mary Tyler

Mary Tyler's *Artists' Books* are mixed media sculptures that use three-dimensional design with words and images. Her works are an accessible form of art because books are portable and common, and also allow for an infinite range of form and content.

In creating her books, Tyler uses a wide variety of painting, photography and printing techniques; handmade papers; and traditional and non-traditional binding methods.

Each book is unique.

EKO

Ellen Kochansky

These small works are intended both as sculptural objects and, in multiples, for corporate and residential walls. Combining humor and seriousness, they represent a long-time quilter's expansion into three dimensions, and apply the same sense of archives, and of repetition. They also draw on Japanese and Native American visual and spiritual traditions. The materials are recycled, and suggest the footprints we leave behind as individuals and as a culture.

Ellen Kochansky has spent 20 years designing one-of-a-kind textile collages for major collections throughout the United States— including the White House Collection—and on several other continents. Since 1984, she has also produced a line of limited-edition contemporary bed quilts, now known as EKO.

A *Bundles*, 1995, recycled textile, metal screen, and kitchen tile, 6" x 6"

B *Bundles*, 1995, recycled cardboard boxes, marble tile, cage screening, plexiglass, and window-shade string, 12" x 12"

A

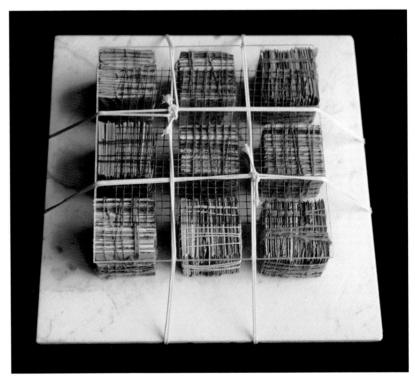

B

Maureen
Burns-Bowie

Maureen Burns-Bowie's organic forms of
hand-built porcelain and slumped glass
reflect psychological and spiritual growth
and development. She has been an artist
for over 20 years, developing unique tools
and techniques to execute her complex
and unusual works.

Burns-Bowie has exhibited in universities,
museums and galleries nationally and internationally, and is the recipient of prestigious
awards, including a number of NEA grants.
She is also listed in several editions of
Who's Who. Ms. Burns-Bowie's works are
one-of-a-kind and limited-edition sculptures,
fountains and production pieces.

Portfolio available.

A *Sunset's Revelation*, porcelain and glass
  sculpture, 24"H x 18"W x 7"D

B *Unity*, porcelain and brass fountain,
  36"H x 20"W x 18"D

A

B

Photos: Wayne Torborg

MIXED & OTHER MEDIA

Josef Caveno

Josef Caveno creates highly functional sculptural elements (top left) for the enrichment of interior design. Cast in hydrostone, Caveno's classically styled pieces feature combinations of sea, air and land creatures suggestive of mythological connections.

Cecilia Denegri

Cecilia Denegri's elegant sculptural cachepots and mirrors (top right) are richly decorated with fabric, knotted and draped in swirling waves. Works are hand finished against a backdrop of color with coppers, ivory, gold or silver—creating an antique look of a tapestry.

Celia & Keith Rice-Jones

Keith and Celia, of Wildrice Studio, create work both individually and collaboratively (bottom). Keith's work hints at esoteric rituals; Celia's traces many roots to the real rituals of everyday domestic activity. There are influences from many cultures, and work ranges from the humble and practical to sculptural statements, from cups and bowls to large house and garden sculptures, figurative gargoyles and architectural forms.

Hans Sipma

Tony Owen

Tony Owen

Silja Lahtinen

Silja's Fine Art Studio

The ancient Lapland shaman created good fortune and riches by using his drum. Now Silja (Talikka) Lahtinen draws ideas from her Scandinavian heritage in creating contemporary drums to bring us good fortune and riches.

Intaglio and silkscreen on leather material — chamois — is a unique working process. Available in any color, and in abstract or realistic images, the drums can be installed in elegant groups in residential or commercial interiors. Many drums have images on both sides. The artist also creates large wall panels with fiber materials and handmade paper on canvas. She exhibits regularly in New York and other U.S. cities, as well as in Paris, France, and Helsinki, Finland.

Commissions accepted. For additional information, please contact the artist.

SHOWN: *My Own Native Feather Coat*, a grouping of three drums, intaglio, silkscreen, chamois, wood- and linocut, with photoetching on chamois, stretched on oval wooden frame, (clockwise from top) 31" × 26"; 28" × 22" and 28" × 22" (reverse view)

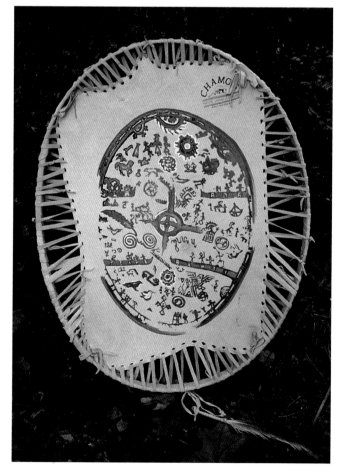

Lea Alboher

Timely Art

A self-taught artisan from Israel, Lea Alboher creates collage clocks full of fantasy and wonder. Lea's eclectic combination of imagery invites you into her world, evoking both feelings of comfort and the unknown. Often blurring the boundaries between indoor and outdoor environments, you may find yourself wandering from a flower garden to a sun-drenched kitchen not knowing where one stops and the other begins.

Living in San Francisco for the past 15 years, Lea collects images which strike her. She cuts and pastes them together and then draws and paints over them using her whimsical touch and undeniable sense of humor. Each clock is unique, and is imbued with her years of experience as a photographer, painter, sculptor, craftswoman, and collector of found objects.

A *Ocean View,* clock, mixed media, 10" × 10"

B *What's Cooking?,* clock, mixed media, 8" × 8"

C *The Kiss of the Zebra,* clock, mixed media, 8" × 8"

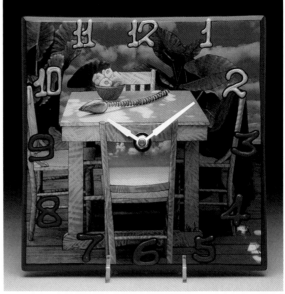

A

B

C

Photos: George Post

Carole Alden Doubek

Doubek & Doubek Studios

Ms. Doubek's creatures have been seen at the National Museum for Women in the Arts, the National Wildlife Art Museum, and—through the Kennedy Center—the Royal Museum in Brussels, Belgium.

In addition to pieces of a definite whimsical nature, she has spent the past year creating realistic, large-scale desert and rain forest installations for children's museums, arboretums and libraries.

Work is primarily hand sewn, painted and airbrushed, using recycled materials.

A *Trouble at Slick Rock*, 1995, polarfleece, polyform clay, fabric paint, 2½' × 4'

B *Lizardo "1"*, 1995, polarfleece, miscellaneous fabrics and found objects, fabric paint, 1' × 3'

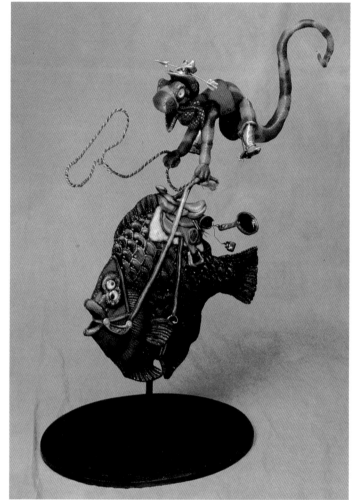

A

Gary Ott

B

Azad

Pat Kazi

Pat Kazi's mixed media sculptures are a composite of historical or fairy tale figures and whimsical creations. Others are based on real ancestors from 19th century Maine.

After making the animals of stoneware clay and the people of porcelain, she embellishes them with antique fabric, beads, fur, wings, and other unique found items.

Ms. Kazi has been in many regional, national, juried and invitational museum shows and is included in several museum collections.

Rhino pull toy, 1995, mixed media, 14"W x 12"H

Joe Hyde

Pleet Collection
Lynda Pleet

Contemporary cats and dogs, ranging from miniature to life-size, have charmed their way into countless galleries and collections nationally.

Adapted from Lynda Pleet's original ceramic sculptures, these pieces are solid cast in porcelainized resin and hand painted in the Pleet Collection studios.

The stylized forms, enhanced by graphic brushwork, capture each animal's unique vitality.

Cats available in many styles and patterns; dogs available in most breeds.

Alice Watterson

A festive collaboration of design, embellishment and personal myth characterizes these engaging figures. Created from bright, hand-woven fabrics and with special attention to detail, each piece is a visual tribute to the enduring strength and beauty in life ... as well as the pleasure inherent in work well made.

SHOWN: *Believer* series, 1995, ironwood bases, 14" to 22"H

Gregg Mastorakos

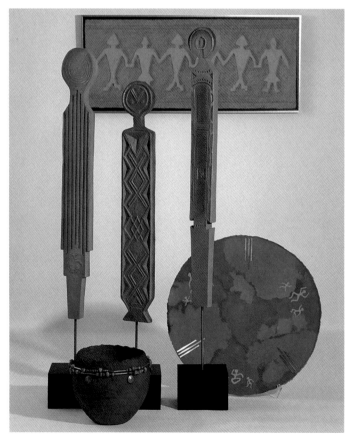

Pat Berrett

Nancy J. Young
Allen Young

The Youngs create original two- and three-dimensional free-standing sculptures and mixed-media wall art. Color preferences and commissions accepted.

Commissions include the U.S. Department of State, AT&T, IBM and American Express.

SHOWN: Hand-cast panel, 20"H x 4'W x 2½"D; mixed-media figures, 4'6" to 5'6" x 4½" to 6"W x 2½"D; vessel, 16"H x 13"Dia; plate, 30"Dia x 2½"D

Anne Mayer Meier
Creative Textures

Anne Mayer Meier has been creating a broad range of contemporary art to complement residential and corporate settings since 1979. Meier's *Ancestors*© and *Old Souls*© are mixed-media figures that evoke man's primitive past using original design and fabrication. Often, found objects are included to enhance the magical qualities of the pieces.

Although fictional in nature, each one-of-a-kind *Ancestor* or *Old Soul* explores cultural, spiritual and folkloric concepts. Meier's new *Spirit Seekers*© (below) and *Playmates*© (not shown) contribute to her study of the feminine aspect.

Contact the artist for further information.

Also see these GUILD publications: *Gallery Edition 1; THE GUILD 4, 5; Designer's Edition 6, 7, 8, 10.*

A *Wisdom Keeper*, from the *Ancestor* series, hand-formed clay face and beads, wood, fabric, leather, feathers, grapevine, mixed-media beads, excelsior and lucite, 2'H

B *Spirit Seekers*, fabric, hand-formed clay face, beads, wire, lucite stands, 15"H

A

B

GLOSSARY OF WOOD & LEATHER TERMS

Marquetry vessels with segmented turnings by Artistry in Wood, photo: ©1994 Wally Hampton

WOOD

BAND SAW A POWER SAW EMPLOYING A CONTINUOUS LOOP OF TOOTHED METAL BAND.

BURL A DOME-SHAPED GROWTH ON THE TRUNK OF A TREE.

HOLTZAPFFEL LATHE A TRADITIONAL WOODTURNING MACHINE WITH CARVING ATTACHMENTS POWERED BY THE LATHE INSTEAD OF BY HAND; USED FOR ORNAMENTAL OR DECORATIVE WORK.

JIG SAW A NARROW SAW MOUNTED VERTICALLY IN A FRAME FOR CUTTING CURVES OR OTHER DIFFICULT LINES.

LAMINATED COMPOSED OF LAYERS BONDED TOGETHER FOR STRENGTH, THICKNESS OR DECORATIVE EFFECT.

MARQUETRY DECORATIVE PATTERNS FORMED WHEN THIN LAYERS OF WOOD (AND SOMETIMES OTHER MATERIALS SUCH AS IVORY) ARE INLAID INTO THE SURFACE OF FURNITURE OR OTHER WOOD PRODUCTS.

MORTISE A NOTCH, HOLE, GROOVE OR SLOT MADE IN A PIECE OF WOOD TO RECEIVE A TENON OF THE SAME DIMENSIONS.

ROUTER A MACHINE WITH A VERTICAL, DRILL-LIKE CUTTER FOR CUTTING DESIGNS INTO WOOD OR FOR DECORATIVELY EDGING IT.

SPALTED NATURALLY DECAYED WOOD WITH DISTINCTIVE MARKINGS; USED FOR ITS DECORATIVE EFFECT.

TENON A PROJECTION ON THE END OF A PIECE OF WOOD.

TURNED WOOD SHAPED BY TOOLS WHILE IT REVOLVES ABOUT A FIXED AXIS, SUCH AS A LATHE. CYLINDRICAL FORMS (DOWELS, RUNGS) AND CIRCULAR DESIGNS (BOWLS) ARE MADE IN THIS WAY.

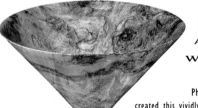

Phil F. Brown created this vividly patterned vessel from a spalted maple burl

LEATHER

BOILING A WATER-FORMING TECHNIQUE IN WHICH LEATHER IS IMMERSED FOR A SHORT TIME IN BOILING WATER, CAUSING THE LEATHER TO BEND AND PUCKER. WHEN DRY, THE LEATHER IS EXTREMELY HARD, THOUGH FRAGILE.

CARVING A DECORATIVE TECHNIQUE IN WHICH THE SURFACE OF THE LEATHER IS CUT WITH A SWIVEL KNIFE AND THE BACKGROUND IS DEPRESSED USING MODELLING TOOLS OR STAMPS. ALSO CALLED INCISING.

GLOSSARY OF WOOD & LEATHER TERMS

CHROME TANNING
A TANNING PROCESS USING SALTS OF CHROMIUM TO MAKE LEATHERS THAT ARE ESPECIALLY SUPPLE AND SUITABLE FOR BAGS, GARMENTS, ETC.

CUIR-BOUILLI
('KWEER-BOO-EE') LITERALLY, BOILED LEATHER. A GENERAL TERM FOR LEATHER THAT IS WATER-FORMED.

EMBOSSING
A DECORATIVE TECHNIQUE IN WHICH A DESIGN IS RAISED IN RELIEF. EMBOSSED LEATHER IS WORKED WITH MODELLING TOOLS ON BOTH HAIR (GRAIN) SIDE AND FLESH (INNER) SIDE.

GLUE-RESIST
A DECORATIVE TECHNIQUE IN WHICH A REMOVABLE GLUE IS APPLIED TO THE LEATHER BEFORE IT IS DYED. THE DYE CANNOT PENETRATE THE GLUE PROTECTED AREAS.

LAMINATING
A TECHNIQUE OF BONDING LAYERS OF LEATHER TOGETHER UNDER PRESSURE FOR STRENGTH, THICKNESS OR VISUAL EFFECT.

LASTING
A WATER-FORMING PROCESS IN WHICH THE DAMP LEATHER IS FORCED OVER A MOLD AND CLAMPED OR NAILED IN PLACE UNTIL DRY. WHEN DRY, THE LEATHER RETAINS THE MOLDED SHAPE.

SADDLE STITCHING
A TWO-HANDED STITCHING TECHNIQUE USING A NEEDLE AT BOTH ENDS OF A SINGLE THREAD. IT PRODUCES A UNIFORM STITCH ON BOTH SIDES OF THE LEATHER.

STAMPING
A TECHNIQUE USING HANDMADE OR COMMERCIAL METAL STAMPS ON DAMP LEATHER TO CREATE A PATTERN OR TO DEPRESS THE BACKGROUND OF A CARVED PIECE.

SPLIT
THE INNER LAYER OF THE LEATHER CUT FROM THE TOP GRAIN PORTION.

SUEDE
A TYPE OF LEATHER IN WHICH THE FLESH SIDE IS BUFFED SMOOTH. SUEDE SPLITS ARE BUFFED ON BOTH SIDES.

J. Todd Barber used water-formed leather for an unusual effect in this sculpted box, photo: Barry O'Hagan

TOOLING
GENERAL NAME GIVEN TO SEVERAL RELATED TECHNIQUES OF WORKING VEGETABLE-TANNED LEATHER TO CREATED EFFECTS OF LOW RELIEF: CARVING, STAMPING, EMBOSSING, ETC.

TOP-GRAIN
THE OUTER SURFACE OF THE HIDE, STILL POSSESSING THE ORIGINAL GRAIN SURFACE; THE HAIR SIDE.

VEGETABLE TANNING
(OR OAK, BARK TANNING) A TANNING PROCESS USING EXTRACTS OF TANNIC ACID. VEGETABLE-TANNED LEATHER IS STRONG, AND SUITABLE FOR BELTS, BAGS, ETC. IT CAN ALSO BE WATER-FORMED.

Linda Sue Eastman's blanket chest incorporates tooling and color applied with an airbrush, photo: Jane Weisbrod

WATER-FORMED
(WET-FORMED) A TECHNIQUE IN WHICH LEATHER IS DAMPENED TO MAKE IT MORE PLIABLE, AND WORKED FREEHAND OR OVER A MOLD OR LAST. WHEN DRY, THE LEATHER WILL RETAIN ITS SHAPE.

FIBER FIBER FIBER

FIBER FIBER FIBER

Rainbow Rugs
by Rose

Rose Marie Patrick

Rose Marie has been weaving for seven years and is a juried member of the Pennsylvania Guild of Craftsmen. Her work can be viewed at her studio and area gift shops.

Her beautifully designed rag rugs are tightly woven of quality cotton fabrics. They are reversible, long-wearing and washable. All items can be hand stenciled to match your decor.

Creations include area or room-size rugs, throw rugs, runners, stair carpet, placemats and table runners.

Items made to your specifications and design.

Photos: Jim Nicolais

Carl T. Chew

The Contemporary Carpet Center

Carl T. Chew limited-edition wool rugs are legendary for their beauty and durability. They are intended for use on the floor. Each rug is handwoven in his small factory, The Contemporary Carpet Center, in Kathmandu, Nepal, using the finest wool, Swiss dyes, and adult weavers.

SHOWN: *Blue 3*, one of a series of rugs depicting koi ponds, 6' x 9', edition of ten

Tom Collicott

Bob Bowné, Neptune, NJ

Cleopatra Steps Out

Kate Mellina
Dave Christopher

Fiber artist Kate Mellina has long been drawn by ancient images: the mystery and sophistication of cave paintings; the grace and vitality of ancient Crete; the spirals, whorls and triangles that magically unite cultures and generations.

Now, Kate and husband Dave Christopher honor these images in *Ancient Icons*, a luxurious collection of handcrafted wool rugs.

Please call for style cards and customization.

SHOWN: *Rock Keeper*, tufted wool rug, color and size options available

Beth Cassidy

Elegant yet durable, Beth Cassidy's line of *Comfort Quilts* infuses a contemporary spirit into the most sophisticated of bed apparel.

These impressionistic spreads are designed in silk, wool, cotton or upholstery fabric, machine pieced and organically quilted. Each is backed in cotton, glazed chintz, or flannel.

Prices range from $30 for a small pillow to $1,100 for a silk, king-size quilt.

A portfolio of this and other lines is always available.

Jeff Brice

"The best *statement on my life* will come when my **clients** tell their **grandchildren** about the time they had their **favorite piece of furniture** made, around the turn of the century. *If things go as planned,* I'll be around to **hear** it."

Michael Jon Flores
Clements, CA

Jennifer Mackey
Chia Jen Studio

Jennifer Mackey of Chia Jen Studio uses sponging, painting, screen printing and appliqué techniques to fashion unique designs. Mackey's works blend European, Mediterranean and Eastern influences.

"My greatest interest is a strong sense of art within the home/public environment," says Mackey, who strives for a very creative and fresh look. Jennifer applies her talents to upholstery fabrics, drapery material, floor coverings, hangings, etc. Her clients are in both the design community and the general public.

Chia Jen Studio offers its designs in natural fiber textiles such as linen, silk, hemp, wool and cotton. Non-toxic, water-based pigments are used; they are colorfast and environmentally sensitive.

Color brochure available.

A Floor canvas, 1992, Pullman estate, 60" x 180"

B Floor canvas (detail), 1992, installation for Consulting Connections

A

B

Photos: Walter Jebbe

Marion Philipsen Shenton

Wind's Edge

For over ten years, Marion Philipsen Shenton has been creating award-winning wall hangings and sculptures out of nylon fabric. The vivid colors and durability of the materials allow her designs to be used in many different applications. Color brochure is available on request.

SHOWN: *Penny's Elephants,* 1994, pieced and appliquéd nylon with rayon tassels, stretched on a graphite frame, 47"W x 42"H, limited edition of 75

Margaret Cusack

Margaret Cusack's stitched hangings reflect her interest in representational imagery, her extensive drawing skills and a striking command of color. Since 1972, she has been creating stitched commissions and portraits for both public and private collections. Her technique is sewing machine appliqué using a wide variety of fabrics and textures.

Commissioned works are in the collections of Yale New Haven Hospital, Seagram's, Aid to Lutheran Association, American Express, and Catholic Medical Center.

SHOWN: *A Time For Hope,* 1995, stitched fabric artwork celebrating the life of Bishop Francis J. Mugavero, 72" x 144"

THIS IS NOT A TIME FOR OPTIMISM THAT SEES NO PROBLEMS, NOR FOR PESSIMISM THAT SEES NO POSSIBILITIES. IT IS A TIME FOR HOPE.

Paul Armbruster

Nancy Moore Bess

The internationally known baskets and wall pieces of Nancy Moore Bess capture details of ancient armor, Japanese folk art and packaging, and African jewelry. Display for the vessels includes Japanese river stones, and bamboo and copper stands. Custom-made lucite boxes frame the wall art, allowing for easy installation and maintenance in public and private sites.

Also see these GUILD publications: *Gallery Edition 1, 2; THE GUILD 4, 5; Designer's Edition 6, 7, 8*

SHOWN: *O-Seibo Baskets II*, collection of the American Craft Museum

D. James Dee

Tina Fung Holder
Fung Holder Designs

Ancient designs from the Amerindians of Guyana are used with modern, industrial materials in Tina Fung Holder's baskets. She utilizes traditional basketry and also incorporates beading and other textile techniques in creating her forms and textures. There is a spiritual bonding of the 'old' and the 'new' within these containers.

Tina Fung Holder also designs and makes non-traditional jewelry. Her work is represented in the collections of the American Craft Museum, the Renwick Gallery of the Smithsonian Institution, and the Wustum Museum.

SHOWN: *Charming Snake*, from the *Amerindiana Series*, 1993, plastic tubing, monofilament, glass beads, 6¼" × 5" × 4½"

Jeff Bayne

Janice Jones
Jones Limited

With patterns inspired by antique textiles and intricate color combinations from nature, these sensual scarves and shawls enchant all who see them. Those who wear them are wrapped in a sense of comfort, a feeling of being 'home.'

These pieces are hand-woven and hand-finished by Janice, a weaver for 25 years who still finds delight in the interaction of color, pattern and the sensation of silk.

Scallop series available in several colors.

SHOWN: *Scallop Scarf*, indigo, 16" x 70"

Bob Barrett

Jill Collier Designs

Elegant textile expressions for both personal adornment and the living environment are created on the handlooms of Jill Collier Designs.

Innovative, award-winning scarves and throws are produced by the union of original weave structures with custom novelty yarns made from a wide variety of fine fibers. The formulas used for combining color, texture and weave produce a unique look in the world of functional fiber!

Jill Collier holds a B.S. in textile design from the Philadelphia College of Textiles and Science, has 15 years experience in the commercial textile industry, and has exhibited her work nationally in museums and galleries.

SHOWN: *Elemental*, hand-woven chenille scarves, 12" x 66"

Betty Kershner
Handpainted Silk

Betty Kershner dyes different weights and textures of silk using resist, hand painting, and shibori techniques. Some garments are pieced and constructed from a palette of colors and textures; others are sewn from the dyed silk.

Betty creates easy-fitting, washable and versatile kimonos, coats, tunics, skirts, blouses and scarves to be worn together or separately.

SHOWN: Shibori coat, pongee, habotai, crinkle georgette with silk frogs and cord ties

Kathy Scrantom

Sue Jarrett

J.H. Warrington
Partridge Hill Studio

J.H. Warrington is a fiber collector who creates windings of multiple strands of unique yarns in an infinite variety of rich colors and textures.

The windings then become hand-knitted hats and vests and hand-woven scarves and rugs that exhibit the innovative character of an experimenter with a strong color and hand sense for fiber work.

Excellent construction standards combine artistic delight with usable durability to ensure a lifetime of enjoyment.

Ronald Salomon
Wildfiber Studio

Through his baskets and vessels, Ronald Salomon pursues his fascination with texture and color. Each piece is designed to be looked at and touched and each piece, throughout the price range, is unique.

Traditional off-loom techniques are combined with both traditional and unusual materials to create baskets and wall pieces that are both functional and decorative.

Loom-woven runners, rugs and blankets are designed to complement the basketry.

Tad Merrick

John Toth

Kim Yost Merck
Rosepath Handwovens

Color and pattern transitions are a major focus of the handwoven scarves designed by Kim Yost Merck. The wonderful drape and feel of the fabric, woven of hand-dyed silk, cotton, and rayon, create a distinctive and elegant scarf.

A 1995 Niche Award winner, Kim sells her work through galleries nationally and at American Craft Council shows in the Southeast.

Contact the artist for additional information.

SHOWN: Collection of *ZigZag* and *Checkerboard Rainbow* scarves

Sue Harmon

Sue Harmon Studios

The artist's hand and eye are evident in each piece created by Sue Harmon Studios.

After five years working in close cooperation with interior designers and galleries, Sue Harmon still finds each creation to be a new challenge. Incorporating her ever-increasing collection of yarns, ribbons, metallics, and other unusual fibers, each throw epitomizes a unique, one-of-a-kind piece of 'art for furniture.'

Selected throws are being shown throughout the country. This year, Sue was available for limited trunk shows.

Sue welcomes collaborations. A limited inventory is always available.

Jeffrey A. Rycus/Rycus Associates Photography

Radlund and Associates, Madison, WI

First Weavers of the Americas

Martina Masaquiza
Rosa María Masaquiza

Natives of a Quechua Indian village renowned for its fine weaving, the Masaquizas offer perhaps the best values in indigenous art today. They hand-dye natural wool with non-toxic Swiss dyes. Their weavings are uncommonly detailed. Tapestry mountings are museum-quality and designed to quiet and warm a room. The pillows are light, large and easily cleaned.

First Weavers is experienced in producing gallery shows and in creating replica and custom works.

Barbara Cade used hand-felted wool to create an oversized *Pansy Bouquet*, photo: Cindy Momchilov

APPLIQUÉ STITCHERY IN WHICH A DESIGN IS CREATED BY SEWING PIECES OF FABRIC OR OTHER MATERIALS TO A FABRIC BACKGROUND.

BATIK (1) A METHOD OF APPLYING DYE TO CLOTH WHICH IS COVERED IN PART WITH A DYE-RESISTANT, REMOVABLE SUBSTANCE SUCH AS WAX. AFTER DYING, THE RESIST IS REMOVED, AND THE DESIGN APPEARS IN THE ORIGINAL COLOR AGAINST THE NEWLY-COLORED BACKGROUND. (2) THE CLOTH ITSELF.

FAILLE A WOVEN COTTON, RAYON OR SILK FABRIC SHOWING A SLIGHT RIBBING.

FELTING (1) FABRIC MADE OF UNSPUN WOOL (SOMETIMES WITH FUR AND OTHER NATURAL OR SYNTHETIC FIBERS) WHICH IS MATTED TOGETHER WITH MOISTURE, HEAT AND PRESSURE. (2) A FABRIC RESEMBLING THIS, SUCH AS HIGHLY NAPPED COTTON.

HAND-SCREENED STENCIL-PRINTED CLOTH TO WHICH ONE OR MORE COLORS ARE APPLIED BY HAND THROUGH STRETCHED, FINE-MESHED 'SCREENS' OF SILK OR ORGANDY. THE MESH IS BLOCKED WHERE COLOR IS NOT WANTED.

HARNESS THE FRAME OF A LOOM UPON WHICH THE HEDDLES ARE PLACED. WARP THREADS ARE DRAWN THROUGH THE EYES OF THE HEDDLES, WHICH MOVE UP AND DOWN AS THE SHUTTLE WITH THE WEFT YARN PASSES BY. THE MOVEMENT OF THE HEDDLES DETERMINES THE PATTERN.

These vibrant batik flowers are by Marilyn Forth, photo: Anthony Potter, Syracuse, NY

GLOSSARY OF FIBER TERMS

Sheila O'Hara 'paints' with a needle and yarn;
this tapestry is titled *Real Escape*

IKAT YARN WHICH IS EITHER TIE-DYED OR PAINTED BEFORE BEING WOVEN INTO FABRIC.

OVERSHOT A DISTINCT WEAVING PATTERN OR THE TECHNIQUE FOR ACHIEVING IT. IT INVOLVES A SPECIAL LOOM THREADING AND THE USE OF HEAVY YARN ALTERNATING WITH FINER YARN IN THE WEFT OR NARROW DIRECTION.

PLANGI WOVEN FABRIC PATTERN-DECORATED BY TIE-DYEING: THAT IS, BY TIEING OR KNOTTING PARTS OF THE FABRIC SO THAT IT WILL NOT ABSORB THE DYE.

RESIST (RESIST DYE) PATTERNING OF YARN OR TEXTILE BY COVERING CERTAIN AREAS, USUALLY WITH LIQUID WAX, BEFORE DYEING.

TAPESTRY A WEFT-FACED FABRIC, OFTEN WITH SLITS WHERE COLORS MEET.

TRAPUNTO DECORATIVE QUILTING IN WHICH THE DESIGN IS OUTLINE-STITCHED IN TWO LAYERS OF FABRIC, THEN PADDED HEAVILY BETWEEN TO FORM A HIGH RELIEF.

WARP THE YARN WHICH RUNS THE LONG WAY IN CLOTH MADE ON A LOOM. IT IS UNDER TENSION DURING WEAVING AND IS USUALLY STRONGER THAN THE 'WEFT' OR 'FILL' YARNS WHICH RUN ACROSS IT.

WEAVING THE PROCESS OF MAKING FABRIC BY INTERLACING A SERIES OF WARP YARNS WITH WEFT YARNS AT RIGHT ANGLES.

WEFT-FACED A TAPESTRY WEAVE IN WHICH THE YARN RUNNING THE SHORT WAY IS DOMINANT IN THE DESIGN.

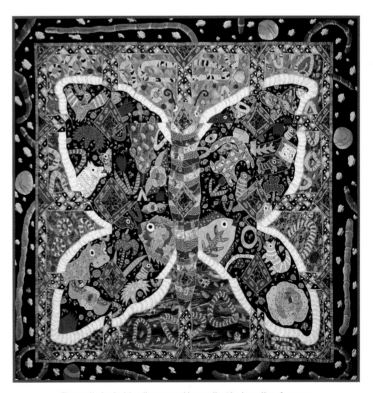

Therese May's playful quilts are machine appliquéd, photo: Mert Carpenter

LIGHTING & FURNITURE

LIGHTING & FURNITURE

Phoenix Studios
Carl Radke

In 1975, Phoenix Studios was founded and dedicated to recapturing the beautiful lusters and colors of glass produced in the United States around the turn of the century.

Carl Radke, owner, designer and glass blower, has been working with glass for 25 years. Working with Carl are Chris Funk, a designer and glass blower with 18 years experience, and Dave Mills, apprentice.

SHOWN: *Large Lamp*, 20" × 10", and *Magnum Cherry Blossom Lamp*, 27" × 14"

Flash Alexander

Ian Raymond Photography

Winnepesaukee Forge, Inc.
David H. Little

The Winnepesaukee Forge Collection of wrought iron by David Little includes distinctive hand-forged furnishings and design accents such as tables, chairs, chandeliers, fireplace accessories, wine racks and drapery hardware.

These pieces reflect David's genuine respect for traditional blacksmithing techniques and attention to detail, and his belief that excellent craftsmanship has strong visual, as well as functional, appeal.

Catalogs available. Private, corporate, architectural and interior commissions are also welcomed.

Pat Wilie Sculptures

Pat Wilie's award-winning works emphasize the element of light. From ceramic sconces and lamps to life-sized painted steel, Wilie's innovation is to combine architecture, color and sculpture.

Portfolio, prices and additional information available upon request.

A & B *Blue Moon Eclipse*, neon between two slip-cast and glazed ceramic disks; transformer and all hardware are housed within the unit. Profile shows how *Eclipse* is mounted at the point of contact with the wall. Eclipse is available in any color neon, but like Henry Ford's Model T, the ceramic face comes only in black, 11½" × 11½" × 5"

C *Woven Sphere* (detail), slip cast and carved ceramic spherical disk creating a spectacular pattern of light, pedestal optional, 15" × 15" × 6"

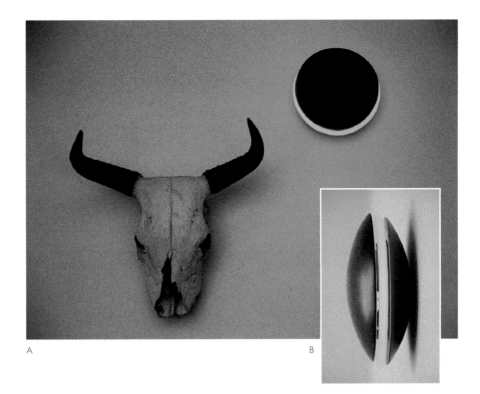

A

B

C

Roger Lee Lewis

Jazz Ranch Studio

Roger Lee Lewis's diverse cultural and educational background is reflected in his illuminated sculpture. The recurrence of Native American themes with strong narrative elements stems from his own tribal identity and a degree in English literature. His experience as an industrial millwright and sculptural metal worker provides him with a wide vocabulary of fabrication techniques.

Roger's work marries 20th century technology to the craft of an earlier America.

Commissions are welcome. Installation is available.

A *Squaretop*, steel, paper, wood, electrical, 27"H

B *Spirit Messengers*, steel, paper, wood, electrical, 63"H

A

B

Hisao Hayashi
Ki no Akari Gallery
JAPAN

Mr. Hayashi's family business is making wood fittings for Japanese-style housing. He now uses the delicately refined *kumiko* joinery technique that is traditionally used in making *shoji* and *fusuma* screens to create superb light fittings for modern interiors. Neither nails nor glue is used in building the frames.

A *Spire*, left: 22"H × 8" × 8"; right: 31"H × 12" × 12"

B *Building*, left: 25"H × 8" × 8"; right: 38"H × 10" × 10"

C Inside of Ki no Akari Gallery

A

B

C

John Clark
John Clark Furniture

John Clark blends traditional furniture forms with historical architectural references to create modern pieces that are fresh yet familiar. His work has appeared in *Fine Woodworking*, *The New York Times*, and *American Craft*.

John earned nis M.F.A. in furniture design from the Program in Artisanry at Boston University. He further developed his work during his tenure as an artist-in-residence at the Penland School of Crafts.

Burning Bench, 1994, dyed curly maple, carved and painted poplar, linen cord, 48" × 22" × 24"

Maynard & Maynard Furnituremakers
Peter Maynard

For more than 22 years, Peter Maynard has been designing and building classic fine furniture in both traditional and contemporary interpretations.

His work has been featured in numerous publications, including *Architectural Digest*, *Interior Design* and *Traditional Home*, which featured Peter and his work in an article titled "20th Century Masters: Five of the Country's Best Furnituremakers."

Also see these GUILD publications: *Gallery Edition 2*; *THE GUILD 5*; *Designer's Edition 6, 8*.

SHOWN: Game table, in closed position, solid curly maple with ebony and rosewood inlays, 30"H × 36"L × 18"D (36"D when opened)

Michael Jon Flores

Michaeljon, Woodworker

Michael Jon has been designing and building heirloom-quality furniture for over 25 years.

His Craftsman-style furniture, constructed with primitive lines for comfort and durability, emphasizes the natural interest of grain, texture and color. Michael Jon also produces a complete line of English garden furniture.

His commissioned work can be seen in museums, galleries and private collections. Numerous awards include Best of Show at Beckman's.

China cabinet, courtesy of the Boudreaux Collection

Covello Photography, Stockton, CA

Richard Sheremeta

Artistic Woodworking

Simple elegance, with a sense of grace and delicacy of form, characterize the unique, non-traditional furniture of this award-winning artist.

Whether it be a hand-carved chair or whimsical accent table, the level of sophistication and craftsmanship in Sheremeta's work distinguishes it as not only functional, but worthy of being admired as pure sculpture.

SHOWN: *Sculpted Rocking Chair #3*, curly maple, 48"H x 20"W x 48"D

CHAIRman of the BOARD
Wolf Sittler

Combine a small fortune in solid maple burl with ergonomic principles, a pleasing design and expert craftsmanship, and the result is a piece of functional sculpture that provides lasting comfort and beauty.

Since chairs are very personal, Wolf makes each one to order and thus customizes each to the needs and desires of its user. His chairs are in daily use in over 100 offices and homes throughout America.

Jerry Anthony

Patrick Leonard
Patrick's Fine Furniture

Patrick Leonard specializes in unique boxes which utilize woods from around the world. The natural colors of the woods he uses are never stained or altered in any way, just protected with a clear durable finish.

The piece pictured here, with its graceful lines and simple beauty, is just one example of Patrick's commitment to functional sculptural art.

SHOWN: Oriental chest of drawers, black walnut, lacewood, 12½"D × 8"W × 14"H

Abby Morrison
Ace Woodwork

Abby Morrison has been creating graceful burlwood vessels and furniture for over 15 years. Each piece is a unique blending of form and function that begins with the innate shape of the burl. The chairs are truly usable sculpture, sensually contoured for seating comfort.

With a strong background in traditional joinery, Morrison welcomes commissions and collaborations of a wide variety, especially those incorporating unusual and burled wood.

Current photos are available for a $15 refundable deposit.

Release, 1995, spalted maple burl, 24"W × 20"D × 7"H

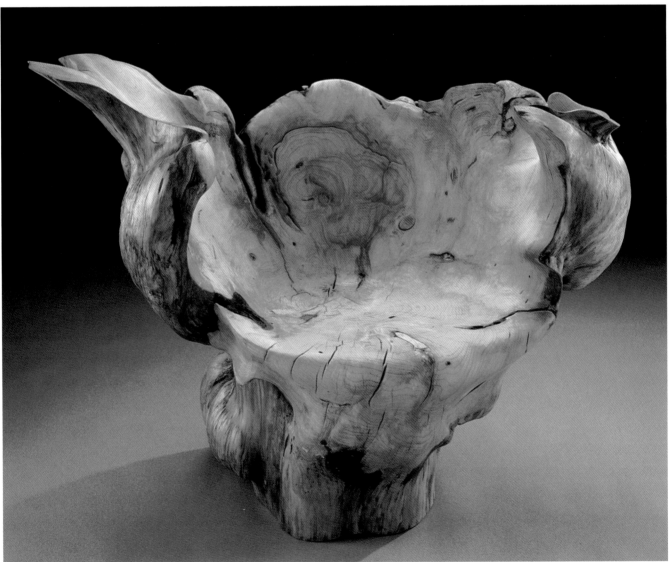

Heart of a Dancer, 1995, spruce burl, 48"W × 34"D × 36"H

Photos: William Thuss

Concepts By J, Inc.

Jay Meepos

Concepts By J has been designing, manufacturing and finishing high-end custom cabinetry, furniture, millwork and architectural woodwork since 1978. Designs cover virtually all styles and periods, traditional and contemporary, and have been installed locally, nationally and internationally.

In addition, Concepts By J has completed several projects for home theaters and entertainment units of all sizes and complexity. The president, Jay Meepos, has done extensive design work in all areas of cabinet and furniture design.

Concepts By J takes pride in producing fine cabinetry for a wide variety of job conditions.

"*The artist develops and uses real creative imaging which combines head and heart. This head-and-heart work creates the finest, richest product that the human being can produce. It is an informative, healing, sublimating work that has the potential to lift one out of the lower self into the larger, free, more creative self. The order and harmony that art can bring is astonishing and sobering.*"

Leroy Wheeler Parker
Lafayette, CA

Jimmy Wray
Key West Woodworks

Key West architectural elements, recovered from old houses and assembled into frames for beveled mirrors, provide a unique stage to see oneself. Colors of the Caribbean are revealed through careful sanding of the many years of layers of old paint.

After receiving a degree in fine arts from the University of South Florida, Jimmy Wray came to Key West, where he has been a designer and woodworker for the past 14 years.

A *I Want to be You*, 24"W × 28½"H

B *23-Carat Marlin*, 22"W × 36"H

C *Carousel Mirror*, 24"W × 30"H

A

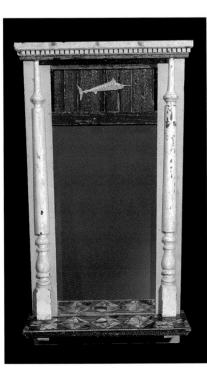

B

C

BUILDING

A CRAFT COLLECTION

By Leslie Ferrin

Leslie Ferrin is the owner and director of Ferrin Gallery at Pinch Pottery, Northampton, MA.

Several years ago, I got a call from clients interested in expanding their collection of contemporary craft. They had sold a number of paintings purchased when they were first married, received a nice return and wanted to 'reinvest' in their new passion: craft.

Meg and Dave had visited the American Craft Museum in New York and purchased a number of books on craft. They were intrigued by the rich variety of work available, as well as the tactile and physical qualities of the pieces they'd seen. They also liked the fact that many craft objects are useful, and could thus be more fully integrated into their lives than two-dimensional artwork.

This was a great opportunity for me to help create and shape a collection. Rarely do I have a chance to work with collectors from the beginning, to help them develop their individual style. I encouraged Dave and Meg to learn more about the field and mentioned several organizations that work with craft collectors (see sidebar). I also urged them to be systematic by first setting up files of artists they were interested in and later documenting their purchases for future reference.

Together, we visited the library of the American Craft Council, in New York City. We looked over books, magazines, catalogs and files of artists' slides, and began to determine taste preferences. They picked up a few subscription cards for magazines and made a short list of books for their own library.

Meg and Dave decided to build their collection around the work of mid-career artists, whose moderate prices would allow them to include a generous selection of artists and

greater number of pieces in the collection. For the artists, support at a mid-point in their career is critical for continued growth; in a very real sense, collectors are their patrons. For the collector, in addition to benevolent feelings of contributing to an artist's career development, there is the intriguing possibility that this artist may go on to become a major name. In such circumstances, a representative or seminal work might become valuable as an investment.

We spent a day visiting galleries, reviewing their 'stables' of artists and introducing Meg and Dave to the gallery directors. My presence helped them meet people and find their way into the back rooms. Meg was a note-taker and collected gallery cards wherever she went. Dave did most of the talking, eliciting a crash course on craft history and biographical information about artists from gallery staff. I had set up appointments in advance and let galleries know that we were

*Jeweler **Thomas Mann** displays an eclectic mix of antique, rustic and contemporary objects and furnishings in his New Orleans kitchen; photo by William Bennett Seitz (from* Hand and Home: The Homes of American Craftsmen, *Bulfinch Press/Little Brown & Company)*

researching, not yet buying. Nonetheless, everyone was friendly and forthcoming with information, knowing that education and sales are inextricably entwined.

We ended the day at the Cub Room, a great SOHO restaurant, and talked about the artists whose work we'd seen. We separated artists into an "A" list (buy now), "B" list (buy at some time), and "C" list (buy if a good piece becomes available).

Artists on the "A" list passed several criteria. First, Meg and Dave loved the work. Second, they felt the price range was appropriate for their budget. And finally, they knew the work had a place in their home and that it would coordinate well with work from other A-list artists.

The "B" list included artists whose work Dave and Meg liked, but — for one reason or another — did not want to include in their collection at this time. Artists were relegated to this category for any of several reasons. In some cases, the price range was high. In others, they wanted to wait for the next series of work, or weren't sure the artist's work would fit comfortably with other pieces in the collection.

The "C" list represented artists whose work they loved, but whose prices were too steep for their budget. We would keep our eyes open for work from these artists that might come up at an auction or as a secondary sale through the artist's primary gallery.

As time went by, I worked for Dave and Meg both through my own gallery and as an intermediary with other galleries. I also occasionally sought pieces from artists directly. When Meg and Dave worked on their own, especially when the artist was unfamiliar to me, they kept me informed about what they found and any purchases they made. It was important to them that the collection retain some sense of cohesiveness. My role was to help them find work that appealed to them

Candlesticks by metalsmith Paul Knoblauch join function with exuberant design; photo by Bruce Miller

and to guide them regarding the appropriateness of an artist or specific piece for the collection. They also used me to help control impulsive buying, though as time went on they trusted their own intuition more and more.

In addition to visiting galleries and studios, we worked with slides and photos, biographical information, catalogs and articles. The artists and galleries that provided the best materials were easiest to review, and often the quality of the materials made a decision simple. Once decisions were made, I arranged the billing, shipping and payments. My fee was a percentage of the sale, sometimes shared with another gallery. Meg and Dave paid my expenses on the road, as well as an hourly rate for administrative work.

Later, as they grew more knowledgeable, my role shifted. I became more of a liaison with artists and galleries, and occasionally orga-

nized presentations of new work. Although I became less involved with decisions as the collection grew, I was rewarded to see Dave and Meg refine their sense of taste. They also introduced me more than once to exciting work and artists with whom I had been unfamiliar.

My own gallery specializes in teapots, and these became a component of Meg and Dave's larger collection. Quite a few artists are exploring this form today, and collecting teapots is a great way to survey the field of ceramics in the vessel tradition. The price range is reasonable and in relation to other media — glass, wood, and even fiber — you can buy major works by established artists without spending a fortune. Meg and Dave displayed their teapots together on wall pedestals similar to the ones in our gallery, and this delightful grouping became the focal point of their dining room.

As their collection grew, I encouraged Meg to organize her notes, keep a record of each purchase, and set up files on favorite artists and galleries. I also suggested that they photograph important pieces in the collection. If they were ever to sell, donate or loan individual works, good documentation and record keeping would enhance value and make a curator's work easier. Good photographs are key to facilitating this kind of exposure for the collection.

Dave and Meg went on several trips to seek out work in various regions of the country. I often helped by sending them to galleries or museums with good collections. They attended the annual SOFA (Sculpture, Objects and Functional Art) Expositions, where they could meet other collectors and see many galleries at one time. They joined the Art Alliance for Contemporary Glass and Friends of Contemporary Ceramics, two organizations that gather regularly, publish a newsletter and organize visits to private collections.

Over the years, Meg and Dave began to collect the work of a few artists in depth, buying several pieces from different periods of the artist's career and continuing to acquire work from each new series. With other artists, they found that one piece seemed to say it all. Although they started with small-scale objects, as their confidence grew, they graduated to art furniture and sculptural forms. Recently, they have worked closely with several artists, commissioning site-specific work for their home. They remain

Hoyman/Browe Studio designs hand-painted tableware "for people who love to eat and laugh"; photo by Tom Liden

committed to buying only what they love, pieces that move them. And over time, they have developed close friendships with many artists whose work they own, as well as dealers and other collectors they've met along the way.

Now that the collection is well established and the original budget spent, Meg and Dave don't buy as frequently as they used to, though we still enjoy regular correspondence. They recently sent me on a wild search for dinnerware and glassware to complement their beautiful, commissioned dining table. We settled on two or three artists whose work could be mixed and matched. Meg has acquired a highly personal collection of narrative jewelry that reflects images and ideas central to their lives. And they both dream of building a home using craft artists wherever possible. This project will no doubt wait until their retirement.

Meg and Dave are imaginary clients, but their story is based on the real experiences of many collectors I've known. Although I don't often have the opportunity to help a collector in all the ways described here, nearly all go through some of this process.

The great part for any collector is the search, the pursuit. Collecting is about setting initial limits of acquisitions, and then bending those limits to add some new, related item or category to the search.

Inquiries from budding collectors are always welcome.

L.F.

FINDING THE ARTWORK

Yes, you're right.

Contemporary Craft is an exceptional portfolio of fine handmade objects and wearable art. But please don't forget its other dimension, the one that really makes it a unique resource.

The following section includes phone numbers for artists represented in this book, as well as the galleries which carry their work. We urge you to dial those numbers for the best possible reasons: to research and invest in outstanding contemporary artwork.

Not every artist represented here lists a personal phone number: Some prefer to work with the doors barred and the phone cord pulled. Others are happy to fill individual phone orders or direct you to additional galleries close to home.

Artists who haven't listed a personal number under their heading (and many who have, as well)· include phone numbers and locations of the galleries which show their work. Do visit these galleries! They offer a quiet, reflective space to view artwork, and usually display several works from a represented artist. Gallery owners are knowledgeable and enthusiastic about the art forms they carry, and can facilitate special orders.

One special note: This year, for the first time, **Contemporary Craft** includes the work of artists from Japan. These fine artisans may be reached through Yuko Yokoyama at THE GUILD JAPAN (TEL 011-81-3-3400-3221; FAX 011-81-3-3400-3201). Yuko, who speaks fluent English, will be happy to answer questions about the artwork and facilitate orders.

As you shop, remember that much of the artwork shown here is one-of-a-kind. That may well mean the vase you fell in love with on page 2 is unavailable. However, it also means that the artist whose work you love has made—or can make—a piece which will be uniquely yours.

That's the beauty of handmade work.

FINDING THE ARTWORK

LEA ALBOHER
See page 93

DETROIT GALLERY OF CONTEMPORARY	DETROIT, MI 313-873-7888
SELDOM SEEN GALLERY	FORT LAUDERDALE, FL 305-522-7556
ORIEL	SOUTH HADLEY, MA 413-532-6469
THE COLLECTOR	MERRICK, NY 516-379-0805
GALLERY ALEXANDER	LA JOLLA, CA 619-459-9433
SANDPEOPLE	HANALEI, HI 808-826-7848
ILONA AND GALLERY	WEST BLOOMFIELD, MI 810-855-4488
ADRIEN LINFORD	NEW YORK, NY 212-628-4500

MICHELE ALEXANDER
See page 30   **ARDEN, NC**
TEL 704-684-5114

GROVEWOOD GALLERY	ASHEVILLE, NC 704-253-7651
CROSSED PALMS GALLERY	BOKEELIA, FL 913-283-2283
ARTCRAFTERS	BUFFALO, NY 716-881-4320
BROWNING ARTWORK	FRISCO, NC 919-995-5538
ZYZYX	BETHESDA, MD 301-493-0297
TRILLIUM GALLERY	LITTLE SWITZERLAND, NC 704-765-0024
FIRST LIGHT GALLERY	CHARLOTTE, NC 704-543-9939
ZYZYX	BALTIMORE, MD 410-486-9785

ALICE VAN DE WETERING DESIGNS
See page 18   **CALVERTON, NY**
FAX 516-727-2023
TEL 516-369-9225

COONLEY GALLERY	PALO ALTO, CA 415-327-4000
GAYLE WILLSON GALLERY	SOUTHAMPTON, NY 516-283-7430
SOUTHWEST CONTEMPORARY JEWELRY	ALBUQUERQUE, NM 505-243-1108

ANDIAMO GLASS DESIGN
See page 57   **REDMOND, WA**
FAX 206-868-2488
TEL 206-868-7168

THE RACHAEL COLLECTION	ASPEN, CO 303-920-1313
STEIN GALLERY	PORTLAND, ME 207-772-9072
VESPERMANN GLASS GALLERY	ATLANTA, GA 404-350-9698
SEEKERS COLLECTION & GALLERY	CAMBRIA, CA 805-927-8626

ARK NY INC.
See page 72

BARNEYS	NEW YORK, NY 212-339-7300
VERTU	DALLAS, TX 214-520-7817
ARTFUL HAND	BOSTON, MA 617-262-9601
TWIST	PORTLAND, OR 503-224-0334
LIPERT INTERNATIONAL	WASHINGTON, DC 202-625-0541
F. GERALD NEW	MORRISTOWN, NJ 201-425-4485

BAIRD METALWORK DESIGNS
See pages 27 and 68   **NEWTON, MA**
PLEASE CONTACT THE ARTIST DIRECTLY   **FAX 617-527-4235**
TEL 617-893-4166

J. TODD BARBER
See page 86   **ALBANY, NH**
PLEASE CONTACT THE ARTIST DIRECTLY   **TEL 603-447-2881**

BARRY GOODMAN AND SON JEWELERS
See page 26   **COLUMBUS, OH**
PLEASE CONTACT THE ARTIST DIRECTLY   **FAX 614-866-0004**
TEL 800-336-1833

CHERYL BATTAGLIA
See page 84-85   **BOSTON, MA**
PLEASE CONTACT THE ARTIST DIRECTLY   **TEL 617-859-0675**

BARBARA BAYNE
See page 20   **NORTH WALES, PA**
TEL 215-699-3983

SANDRA COLLINS, INC	BIRMINGHAM, MI 313-642-4795
GUILFORD HANDCRAFTS, INC.	GUILFORD, CT 203-453-5947
CRAFT ALLIANCE	ST. LOUIS, MO 314-725-1177
THE REAL MOTHER GOOSE GALLERY	PORTLAND, OR 503-223-3737
HIGH GLOSS	HOUSTON, TX 713-468-2915

STEVI BELLE
See page 24   **TAYLORVILLE, IL**
FAX 217-287-7232
TEL 217-824-9375

SAN ANSELMO ART GLASS GALLERY	SAN ANSELMO, CA 415-457-2082
BEADWORKS	BOSTON, MA 617-247-7227
ARTS AFIRE GLASS GALLERY	ALEXANDRIA, VA 703-838-9785
SABLE V FINE ART GALLERY	WIMBERLEY, TX 512-847-8975
BEAD IT!	BLOOMINGTON, MN 612-858-8612
BEAD IT!	CHICAGO, IL 312-561-9683
EASTERN ILLINOIS UNIVERSITY	CHARLESTON, IL 217-581-3410
BEAD IT!	CHICAGO, IL 312-561-9683

NANCY MOORE BESS
See page 107
PLEASE CONTACT THE ARTIST DIRECTLY

NEW YORK, NY
FAX 212-633-1844
TEL 212-691-2821

BIRDS AND BEASTS
See page 71

AMES, IA
TEL 515-233-1372

OCTAGON CENTER FOR THE ARTS
AMES, IA
515-232-5331

DOMINIQUE BLANCHARD
See page 49

SANTA CLARITA, CA
FAX 805-251-3031
TEL 805-251-3031

RUMORS
NEW ORLEANS, LA
504-525-0292

IMAGE OF THE CULTURE
PALO ALTO, CA
415-342-0621

ANNELEE GALLERY
GLENWOOD, IL
708-757-7100

JUDIE BOMBERGER
See page 73

NOVATO, CA
FAX 415-883-9306
TEL 415-883-3072

SPIRALS
PALO ALTO, CA
415-324-1155

GRAPHIC'S GALLERY
BALBOA ISLAND, CA
714-673-2220

NEW MORNING GALLERY
ASHEVILLE, NC
704-274-2831

SOHO SOUTH
MEMPHIS, TN
901-767-7070

ACCENTRICS LTD
MEQUON, WI
414-241-9292

SIGNATURE STORES INC.
MASHPEE, MA
508-539-0029

TIMOTHY'S GALLERY
WINTER PARK, FL
407-629-0707

SUSAN EILEEN BURNES
See page 35

BRECKSVILLE, OH
FAX 216-526-0874
TEL 216-838-5955

GORDON BEALE FRANK GALLERY
CLEVELAND, OH
216-421-0677

RAINBOWERS
HUDSON, OH
216-467-0259

DUDA GALLERY
BRECKSVILLE, OH
216-526-3210

MAUREEN BURNS-BOWIE
See page 90
PLEASE CONTACT THE ARTIST DIRECTLY

BLOOMINGTON, MN
TEL 612-828-6078

CALIFORNIA GLASS STUDIO
See pages 58 and 63

SACRAMENTO, CA
FAX 916-925-9370
TEL 916-925-9322

OVERWHELMED
BOCA RATON, FL
407-368-0078

ARTFUL HAND
BOSTON, MA
617-262-9601

GLASS CANVAS GALLERY INC.
SAINT PETERSBURG, FL
813-821-6767

(Listing continues)

PETRI'S
SAUSALITO, CA
415-332-2225

FREE FLIGHT GALLERY
DALLAS, TX
214-701-9566

PHOENIX RISING GALLERY
SEATTLE, WA
206-728-2332

CBL FINE ART
WEST ORANGE, NJ
201-736-7776

INTERNATIONAL VILLA
DENVER, CO
303-333-1524

CAROL GREEN STUDIO
See page 45
PLEASE CONTACT THE ARTIST DIRECTLY

PERRYSBURG, OH
FAX 419-872-0589
TEL 419-872-0589

BETH CASSIDY
See page 104

SEATTLE, WA
FAX 206-706-0406
TEL 206-783-6226

UNDERCOVER QUILTS
SEATTLE, WA
206-622-6382

BUNNELL ST. GALLERY
HOMER, AK
907-235-2662

JOSEF CAVENO
See page 91

NEW WESTMINSTER, BC CANADA
FAX 604-540-1062
TEL 604-521-7887

THREE GRACES INC.
VANCOUVER, BC CANADA
604-254-4212

CHAIRMAN OF THE BOARD
See page 122

AUSTIN, TX
FAX 512-447-2150
TEL 512-447-2150

AN AMERICAN CRAFTSMAN
NEW YORK, NY
212-399-2555

CARL T. CHEW
See page 103

SEATTLE, WA
FAX 206-527-0173
TEL 800-644-6246

MIA GALLERY
SEATTLE, WA
206-467-8283

DECOR INTERNATIONAL, INC
BOSTON, MA
617-262-1529

BRANSON BOUTIQUE
KENTFIELD, CA
415-925-1850

CYNTHIA CHUANG AND ERH-PING TSAI
See page 34
PLEASE CONTACT THE ARTIST DIRECTLY

FOREST HILLS, NY
FAX 718-575-9480
TEL 718-793-4225

JOHN CLARK
See page 120

PENLAND, NC
FAX 704-765-7510
TEL 704-765-7510

SANSAR GALLERY
WASHINGTON, DC
202-244-4448

MEREDITH GALLERY
BALTIMORE, MD
301-837-3575

FINDING THE ARTWORK

CLEOPATRA STEPS OUT
See page 103
PLEASE CONTACT THE ARTIST DIRECTLY
ASBURY PARK, NJ
TEL 908-774-6306

CONCEPTS BY J, INC.
See page 124
PLEASE CONTACT THE ARTIST DIRECTLY
LOS ANGELES, CA
FAX 213-564-4332
TEL 212-564-9988

VINCE CRAFT
See page 32
SAUSALITO, CA
TEL 415-332-5221

OSHER OSHER GALLERY	LYNDHURST, OH 216-646-9191
LASTING INDULGENCE	NEW ORLEANS, LA 504-525-2440
EARTHWORKS	LOS ALTOS, CA 415-948-5141
MEADOWLARK GALLERY	CORTE MADERA, CA 415-924-2210
SOMETHING/ANYTHING	SAN FRANCISCO, CA 415-441-8003
ATYPIC GALLERY	MILWAUKEE, WI 414-351-0333
FREE FLIGHT GALLERY	DALLAS, TX 214-701-9566
SAVAS GALLERY	MILL VALLEY, CA 415-380-8098

BOOTS CULBERTSON
See page 45
SARASOTA, FL
TEL 941-355-3604

| ART UPTOWN, INC. | SARASOTA, FL 941-955-5409 |
| VINCENT WILLIAM GALLERY INC. | ST. PETE BEACH, FL 813-363-1334 |

MARGARET CUSACK
See page 106
PLEASE CONTACT THE ARTIST DIRECTLY
BROOKLYN, NY
TEL 718-237-0145

DANCING FIRE STUDIO
See page 50
NEWNAN, GA
TEL 770-251-7876
TEL 770-502-8760

| EDGE OF THE WORLD GALLERY | ATLANTA, GA 404-249-7752 |
| THE RED DOOR GALLERY | CARROLLTON, GA 770-830-0025 |

FRED DANFORTH
See page 68
MIDDLEBURY, VT
FAX 802-388-0099
TEL 800-222-3142

PHOENIX RISING GALLERY	SEATTLE, WA 206-728-2332
PERRY SHERWOOD FINE ART	PETOSKY, MI 616-348-5079
PROMENADE GALLERY	BEREA, KY 606-986-1609
HUNTER UNLIMITED	SANTA BARBARA, CA 805-899-0007
STUDIO B	FREDERICKSBURG, TX 210-997-4547
MACKEREL SKY GALLERY	E. LANSING, MI 517-351-2211
ICARUS	NEWBURYPORT, MA 508-463-9246
AFTER THE RAIN	NEW YORK, NY 212 431 1011

KRISTINE DANIELSON
See page 30
PINCKNEY, MI
TEL 313-426-3439

PHOENIX RISING GALLERY	SEATTLE, WA 206-728-2332
ARIANA GALLERY	ROYAL OAK, MI 810-546-8810
SILVERSCAPE DESIGNS	NORTHAMPTON, MA 413-253-3324
SELDOM SEEN GALLERY	FORT LAUDERDALE, FL 305-522-7556
16 HANDS GALLERY	ANN ARBOR, MI 313-761-1110
ANGELHEART	NEWTOWN, PA 215-968-1614
ARTISANS THREE	SPRING HOUSE, PA 215-643-4504
METALWORKS	PHILADELPHIA, PA 215-625-2640

DAVID CHANGAR CERAMIC DESIGNS
See page 50
NEW YORK, NY
FAX 718-842-6965
TEL 718-842-6362

MUD SWEAT & TEARS EAST	NEW YORK, NY 212-570-6868
WAVE	NEW HAVEN, CT 203-782-6212
LEKAE GALLERIES	SCOTTSDALE, AZ 602-874-2624

DEBRA DEMBOWSKI
See page 33
MILWAUKEE, WI
TEL 414-541-3085

EDGEWOOD ORCHARD GALLERIES	FISH CREEK, WI 414-868-3579
THE GOOD WORKS GALLERY	GLEN ELLYNE, IL 708-858-6654
LINDSEY GALLERY	OAK PARK, IL 708-386-5272
EARTH SPIRITS	PALM DESERT, CA 619-779-8766
ART RESOURCES GALLERY	EDINA, MN 612-922-1770
ART RESOURCES GALLERY	SAINT PAUL, MN 612-222-4431
SIGNATURE	WEST DES MOINES, IA 515-277-5865

CECILIA DENEGRI
See page 91
NEW WESTMINSTER, BC
FAX 604-540-1062
TEL 604-521-7887

| TRUDY VAN DOP GALLERY | NEW WESTMINSTER, BC CANADA 604-521-7887 |

JUDY DITMER
See page 81
PLEASE CONTACT THE ARTIST DIRECTLY
PIQUA, OH
TEL 513-773-1116

CAROLE ALDEN DOUBEK
See page 94
PLEASE CONTACT THE ARTIST DIRECTLY
SALT LAKE CITY, UT
TEL 801-487-1410

LYNN DURYEA
See page 43

PORTLAND, ME
TEL 207-767-7113

BLUE HERON GALLERY	DEER ISLE, ME 207-348-6051
LEIGHTON GALLERY	BLUE HILL, ME 207-374-5001
HANDWORKS	BLUE HILL, ME 207-374-5613
SAWYER STREET GALLERY	S. PORTLAND, ME 207-767-7113
THOS. MOSER	PORTLAND, ME 207-774-3791
GAYLE WILLSON GALLERY	SOUTHAMPTON, NY 516-283-7430

EKO
See page 89

PICKENS, SC
FAX 864-868-4250
TEL 864-868-9749

GALLERY WDO	CHARLOTTE, NC 704-333-9123
LLYN STRONG	GREENVILLE, SC 803-233-5900

ENHANCEMENTS
See page 69

SAN MARCOS, CA
TEL 619-744-8099

ADESSO, LTD	HIGHLAND PARK, IL 708-433-8525
THE GUGGENHEIM MUSEUM	NEW YORK, NY 212-423-3500
GRAND JURY	BETHESDA, MD 301-530-7982
THE IMP	SANTA MONICA, CA 310-917-3320
POSITIVE IMAGES	AUSTIN, TX 512-472-1831
THE PAINTED BIRD	SUTTON'S BAY, MI 616-271-3050
NEWBILL COLLECTION	SEASIDE, FL 904-231-4500
CASCABEL	SCARSDALE, NY 914-725-8922

FIRST WEAVERS OF THE AMERICAS
See page 111
PLEASE CONTACT THE ARTIST DIRECTLY

LAWRENCE, KS
FAX 913-838-4486
TEL 800-571-0156

BILL FITZGIBBONS
See page 46
PLEASE CONTACT THE ARTIST DIRECTLY

SAN ANTONIO, TX
FAX 210-826-0223
TEL 210-826-0223

MICHAEL JON FLORES
See page 121
PLEASE CONTACT THE ARTIST DIRECTLY

CLEMENTS, CA
TEL 209-763-5713

GB JEWELRY
See page 19

LINCOLN, NE
FAX 402-475-1300
TEL 402-475-5850

SIGNATURE STORES INC.	MASHPEE, MA 508-539-0029
FAIRCHILD & CO.	SANTA FE, NM 505-984-1419
THE REAL MOTHER GOOSE GALLERY	PORTLAND, OR 503-223-3737

(Listing continues)

DE NOVO	PALO ALTO, CA 415-327-1256
CONCEPTS	CARMEL, CA 408-624-0661
A PLACE ON EARTH	STUART, FL 407-283-9556
DEL MANO GALLERY	LOS ANGELES, CA 310-476-8508
GALLERY 500	ELKINS PARK, PA 215-572-1203

MARLENA GENAU
See page 32

ORINDA, CA
TEL 510-254-2498

ACCI	BERKELEY, CA 510-843-2527
WEBSTERS	ASHLAND, OR 503-482-9801
GWENDOLYN'S AT WHISTLING SWAN	FISH CREEK, WI 414-868-3602
THE ART OF CRAFT	DENVER, CO 303-292-5564
GUILFORD HANDCRAFTS, INC.	GUILFORD, CT 203-453-5947
DEL MANO GALLERY	LOS ANGELES, CA 310-476-8508

JAN D. GJALTEMA
See pages 22-23

THE WORKS GALLERY	PHILADELPHIA, PA 215-922-7775
THREE ROOMS UP	EDINA, MN 612-922-7231
CONTEMPORARY MUSEUM SHOP	HONOLULU, HI 808-523-3447
THE MODERN OBJECT	COLUMBUS, OH 614-461-9114
GRAND CENTRAL GALLERY	TAMPA, FL 813-254-4977
CLAY AND FIBER	TAOS, NM 505-758-8093
CRAFT ALLIANCE	ST. LOUIS, MO 314-725-1177
DEL MANO GALLERY	LOS ANGELES, CA 310-476-8508

SUE HARMON
See page 111
PLEASE CONTACT THE ARTIST DIRECTLY

COLUMBUS, OH
FAX 614-231-8844
TEL 614-231-9223

THE HARRINGTON COLLECTION, LTD.
See page 19
PLEASE CONTACT THE ARTIST DIRECTLY

ESTES PARK, CO
TEL 303-747-2515

HISAO HAYASHI
See page 119
PLEASE CONTACT THE ARTIST
c/o YUKO YOKOYAMA, JOMON-SHA

TOKYO, JAPAN
FAX 011-81-3-3400-3201
TEL 011-81-3-3400-3221

KI NO AKARI GALLERY	YONEZAWA, YAMAGATA PREF., JAPAN TEL 011-81-238-23-9376

CATHARINE HIERSOUX
See page 46
PLEASE CONTACT THE ARTIST DIRECTLY

BERKELEY, CA
TEL 510-524-8005

FINDING THE ARTWORK

TINA FUNG HOLDER
See page 107
PLEASE CONTACT THE ARTIST DIRECTLY

WASHBURN, WI
TEL 715-373-2050

HULET GLASS
See page 62

CARLYN GALERIE	DALLAS, TX 214-368-2828
RASBERRYS	YOUNTVILLE, CA 707-944-9211
KOHLER ARTS CENTER	KOHLER, WI 414-452-8602
THE GLASS EYE	SEATTLE, WA 800-237-6961
IMPULSE	PROVINCETOWN, MA 508-487-1154
JOANNE'S STAINED GLASS	TRUCKEE, CA 916-587-1280
BERTRAM M. COHEN	BOSTON, MA 617-247-9093
SOMERHILL GALLERY	CHAPEL HILL, NC 919-968-8868

IDELLE HAMMOND-SASS DESIGN
See page 18

ANN ARBOR, MI
TEL 313-741-4441

GALLERY GOLDSMITHS	HOUSTON, TX 713-961-3552
PHOENIX RISING GALLERY	SEATTLE, WA 206-728-2332
LLYN STRONG	GREENVILLE, SC 803-233-5900

JMML DESIGNS
See page 27

MINNEAPOLIS, MN
TEL 612-729-1458

WOLFARD & COMPANY	SANTA ROSA, CA 707-542-7526
ELDERBERRY COLLECTION	WEST DES MOINES, IA 515-271-5045
CELEBRATION DESIGNS	SAINT PAUL, MN 612-690-4344
NORTHFIELD ARTS GUILD	NORTHFIELD, MN 507-645-8877
ARTISANS ALLEY	NIAGARA FALLS, NY 716-282-0196
RAINBOW HARVEST	DUCK, NC 919-261-5949

JAN JACQUE
See page 42
PLEASE CONTACT THE ARTIST DIRECTLY

LIVONIA, NY
TEL 716-346-6772

JAMES J. DURANT ENTERPRISES
See page 71
PLEASE CONTACT THE ARTIST DIRECTLY

NEWPORT BEACH, CA
FAX 714-966-9229
TEL 714-673-5625

JEREMY LAWRENCE DESIGN
See page 60
PLEASE CONTACT THE ARTIST DIRECTLY

PORTLAND, OR
TEL 503-635-1881

JILL COLLIER DESIGNS
See page 108

BRISTOL, RI
FAX 401-254-0751
TEL 401-254-0751

ARTFUL HAND	BOSTON, MA 617-262-9601
NANCY MARGOLIS GALLERY	PORTLAND, ME 207-775-3822
HARLLEE GALLERY	HIGHLANDS, NC 704-526-2083
MINDSCAPE	EVANSTON, IL 708-864-2660
THE CLAY POT	BROOKLYN, NY 718-788-6564

JANICE JONES
See page 108
PLEASE CONTACT THE ARTIST DIRECTLY

BRADFORD, ME
TEL 207-327-1462

JUNO SKY STUDIO
See page 87

FINDLAY, OH
FAX 419-423-9907
TEL 419-423-9591

MARY BELL GALLERIES	CHICAGO, IL 312-642-0202
MILLER GALLERY	CINCINNATI, OH 513-871-4420

ETSUKO KAMIJO
See page 82
PLEASE CONTACT THE ARTIST
C/o YUKO YOKOYAMA, JOMON-SHA

TOKYO, JAPAN

FAX 011-81-3-3400-3201
TEL 011-81-3-3400-3221

SUYA GALLERY	KYOTO, JAPAN TEL-011-81-75-211-7700

PAT KAZI
See page 95

DON DRUMM STUDIOS & GALLERY	AKRON, OH 216-253-6268
D. MORGAN GALLERY	CONYERS, GA 404-922-4554
TIDELINE GALLERY	REHOBOTH BEACH, I, DE 302-227-4444
ARTSI PHARTSI	TAMPA, FL 813-832-2787
DISCOVERIES	MANAYUNK, PA 215-482-1117
DISCOVERIES	READING, PA 215-372-2595
ARIES FINE AMERICAN CRAFTS	OGUNQUIT, ME 207-646-5597
SILVIA ULLMAN GALLERY	CLEVELAND, OH 216-231-2008

BETTY KERSHNER
See page 109

SEWANEE, TN
TEL 615-598-5723

FOLK ART CENTER	ASHEVILLE, NC 704-298-7928
MIDLAND CRAFTERS	PINEHURST, NC 910 295-6156
OAKS GALLERY	DILLSBORO, NC 704-586-6542
GROVEWOOD GALLERY	ASHEVILLE, NC 704-253-7651
PARKWAY CRAFT CENTER	BLOWING ROCK, NC 704-295-7938
ARROWCRAFT SHOP	GATLINBURG, TN 615-436-4604
EXPRESSIONS GALLERY	YARDLEY, PA 215-321-7433

SILJA LAHTINEN
See page 92
PLEASE CONTACT THE ARTIST DIRECTLY

MARIETTA, GA
FAX 770-992-8380
TEL 770-992-8380

ELLIOT LANDES
See page 80

WINTERS, CA
FAX 916-795-0428
TEL 916-795-2648

AN AMERICAN CRAFTSMAN	NEW YORK, NY 212-399-2555
LEGENDS	SONOMA, CA 707-939-8100
ARTFUL HAND GALLERIES	ORLEANS, MA 617-255-2969
CITY WOODS	HIGHLAND PARK, IL 708-432-9393
DIAMOND TANITA GALLERY	CRESTED BUTTE, CO 303-349-0940
THE REAL MOTHER GOOSE GALLERY	PORTLAND, OR 503-223-3737
AMERICAN CRAFT MUSEUM	NEW YORK, NY 212-956-3535
THE COLLECTOR	MERRICK, NY 516-379-0805

ROBERT B. LASH
See page 83
PLEASE CONTACT THE ARTIST DIRECTLY

ELLSWORTH, ME
FAX 207-667-7365
TEL 207-667-1046

LAURA PESCE GLASS
See page 25

TUCSON, AZ
FAX 602-622-4046
TEL 602-624-0343

PHILABAUM GLASS STUDIO	TUCSON, AZ 602-884-7604
OBSIDIAN GALLERY	TUCSON, AZ 602-577-3598
ARIANA GALLERY	ROYAL OAK, MI 810-546-8810
ALIANZA CONTEMPORARY CRAFTS	BOSTON, MA 617-262-2385
STEPHEN FELLERMAN	SHEFFIELD, MA 413-229-8533
STEIN GALLERY	PORTLAND, ME 207-772-9072
REFLECTIONS GLASS GALLERY	GENEVA, SWITZERLAND
VIRGINIA BREIER GALLERY	SAN FRANCISCO, CA 415-929-7173

PATRICK LEONARD
See page 122
PLEASE CONTACT THE ARTIST DIRECTLY

WASHINGTON, PA
TEL 412-222-6943

ROGER LEE LEWIS
See page 118

PAGOSA SPRINGS, CO
TEL 970-264-2925

TERMAR GALLERY	DURANGO, CO 970-247-3728
ABBEY LANE GALLERY	CREEDE, CO 719-658-2736
BRISTOL GALLERY	DENVER, CO 303-620-9822
SPIRITS IN THE WIND GALLERY	GOLDEN, CO 303-279-1192

SERGIO LUB
See page 29

WALNUT CREEK, CA
FAX 510-932-4643
TEL 510-932-5377

DOLPHIN DREAMS	WALNUT CREEK, CA 510-933-2342
HARBOUR TOWN CRAFTS	HILTON HEAD, SC 803-671-3643
ART GLASS ALCOVE	SAUGATUCK, MI 616-857-1854
AMERICAN ARTISAN, INC	NASHVILLE, TN 615-298-4691
PEOPLE'S POTTERY	ITHACA, NY 607-277-3597
TERRY IVORY	STONE HARBOUR, NJ 609-967-4138
FIREWORKS GALLERY	SEATTLE, WA 206-282-8707

JENNIFER MACKEY
See page 105
PLEASE CONTACT THE ARTIST DIRECTLY

SCOTIA, CA
FAX 707-764-2505
TEL 707-764-5877

KIRA J. MAER-LYN
See page 28

MADISON, WI
TEL 608-255-6284

MADISON ART CENTER	MADISON, WI 608-257-0158
MCMILLAN GALLERY	MADISON, WI 608-238-6501
LITTLE LUXURIES	MADISON, WI 608-255-7372
D. HANKO'S	SUGARLAND, TX 713-980-1023
BEADS OF PARADISE	PAIA MAUI, HI 808-579-9459

MARKROY STUDIO
See page 60

PINCONNING, MI
TEL 517-879-5720

MOUNTAIN CRAFT GALLERY	WHISTLER WAY, BC CANADA 604-932-5001

FINDING THE ARTWORK

DAVID MARSON
See page 29
FAYETTEVILLE, AR
TEL 501-444-0300

THE BIBELOT SHOPS	ST. PAUL, MN 612-646-5651
BLUESTEM MISSOURI CRAFTS	COLUMBIA, MO 314-442-0211
SABLE V FINE ART GALLERY	WIMBERLEY, TX 512-847-8975
CLAY PIGEON	SEDONA, AZ 520-282-2845
JOHNSTON GALLERY	MINERAL POINT, WI 608-087-3787
BIER POTTERY	CHARLLEVOIX, MI 616-547-2288
EXPRESSLY WOOD	EVANSTON, IL 708-869-7060
PLEASURES	PARK CITY, UT 801-649-5733

MAYNARD & MAYNARD FURNITUREMAKERS
See page 120
PLEASE CONTACT THE ARTIST DIRECTLY
S. ACWORTH, NH
FAX 603-835-2969
TEL 603-835-2969

CHARLES E. MEDLIN
See page 26
PLEASE CONTACT THE ARTIST DIRECTLY
YORK, NC
TEL 803-684-1446

NANCEE MEEKER
See page 39
RHINECLIFF, NY
FAX 914-876-3118
TEL 914-876-3119

THE WORKS GALLERY	PHILADELPHIA, PA 215-922-7775

ANNE MAYER MEIER
See page 97
LONGWOOD, FL
TEL 407-332-6713

NEW MORNING GALLERY	ASHEVILLE, NC 704-274-2831
LIMITED ADDITIONS	ASPEN, CO 970-925-7112
PIECES	HIGHLAND PARK, IL 708-432-2137
TIMOTHY'S GALLERY	WINTER PARK, FL 407-629-0707
ARTS AND ARTISANS, LTD.	CHICAGO, IL 312-855-9220
DESIGN COLLABORATION	DENVER, CO 303-825-6353
AVALON GALLERY	ROCKY RIVER, OH 216-331-3776
ELEANOR'S CRAFT GALLERY	ENGLEWOOD, NJ 201-816-7376

MELODIOUS
See page 80
PORTLAND, ME
FAX 207-774-2810
TEL 207-774-5519

APPALACHIAN SPRING	FALLS CHURCH, VA 703-533-0930
AMERICAN ARTISAN, INC	NASHVILLE, TN 615-298-4691
ENGEL GALLERY	EAST HAMPTON, NY 516-324-6462
CITY WOODS	HIGHLAND PARK, IL 708-432-9393
SUN UP GALLERY	WESTERLY, RI 401-596-0800
AMERICAN CRAFTWORKS	BOCA RATON, FL 407-362-4220
FRAGILE	ATLANTA, GA 404-257-1323
ZYZYX	BETHESDA, MD 301-493-0297

KIM YOST MERCK
See page 110
BRUNSWICK, GA
TEL 912-267-7920

RAGAZZI'S FLYING SHUTTLE	SEATTLE, WA 206-343-9762
STUDIO 40	WH SULPHUR SPRINGS, WV 304-536-4898
MAPLE GROVE GALLERY	FISH CREEK, WI 414-839-2693
GROVEWOOD GALLERY	ASHEVILLE, NC 704-253-7651

MESOLINI GLASS STUDIO
See page 58
BAINBRIDGE ISLAND, WA
FAX 206-842-7133
TEL 206-842-7133

NEW WEST GALLERY	DURANGO, CO 303-259-5777
HIGH SPIRITS	WENATCHEE, WA 509-633-7798
LE CHERCHE-MIDI	NANTUCKET, MA 508-228-7600
SOCIETY OF ARTS & CRAFTS	BOSTON, MA 617-266-1810
MESOLINI & AMICI	SEATTLE, WA 206-587-0275
ADAM WHITNEY GALLERY	OMAHA, NE 402-393-1051
MATERIAL POSSESSIONS	CHICAGO, IL 312-280-4885
AMALGAMATED	NEW YORK, NY 212-691-8695

METALWEAVINGS
See page 75
PLEASE CONTACT THE ARTIST DIRECTLY
CARRIZOZO, NM
TEL 505-648-2313

ABBY MORRISON
See page 123
ROCKLAND, ME
FAX 207-594-2975
TEL 207-594-1448

HARBOR SQUARE GALLERY	ROCKLAND, ME 207-594-8700
MARK MILLIKEN GALLERY	NEW YORK, NY 212-534-8802

MYERS GONDEK DESIGN
See page 20
MILWAUKEE, WI
TEL 414-264-5836

LANGMAN GALLERY	WILLOW GROVE, PA 215-657-8333
METALWORKS	PHILADELPHIA, PA 215-625-2640
EXPRESSIONS GALLERY	YARDLEY, PA 215-321-7433
CEDANNA GALLERY & STORE	SAN FRANCISCO, CA 415-474-7152

(Listing continues)

NANCY GOODENOUGH, GLASS ARTIST
See page 16

SAN FRANCISCO, CA
TEL 415-759-5105

MINDSCAPE — EVANSTON, IL — 708-864-2660

KITTRELL/RIFFKIND ART GLASS — DALLAS, TX — 214-239-7957

SAN ANSELMO ART GLASS GALLERY — SAN ANSELMO, CA — 415-457-2082

BEADWORKS — BOSTON, MA — 617-247-7227

HANSON GALLERIES — HOUSTON, TX — 713-984-1242

CREATIVE INSPIRATIONS GALLERY — FT. LAUDERDALE, FL — 954-525-1870

DAVID NEW-SMALL
See page 56

VANCOUVER, BC CANADA
TEL 604-681-6730

WHITEBIRD — CANNON BEACH, OR — 503-436-2681

NOUROT GLASS STUDIO
See page 59

APPALACHIAN SPRING — FALLS CHURCH, VA — 703-533-0930

MARSHALL FIELD'S — MINNEAPOLIS, MN — 612-307-5871

CORNING MUSEUM SHOP — CORNING, NY — 607-974-8271

HANSON GALLERIES — HOUSTON, TX — 713-984-1242

DETROIT INSTITUTE OF THE ARTS — DETROIT, MI — 313-833-3924

PHOENIX RISING GALLERY — SEATTLE, WA — 206-728-2332

NORDSTROM'S — VARIOUS LOCATIONS,

CHIKAKO OGATA
See page 43
PLEASE CONTACT THE ARTIST
c/o YUKO YOKOYAMA, JOMON-SHA

TOKYO, JAPAN
FAX 011-81-3-3400-3201
TEL 011-81-3-3400-3221

MICHAEL AND SUSAN OVERSTRÖM
See page 34
PLEASE CONTACT THE ARTIST DIRECTLY

CLARKESVILLE, GA
FAX 706-754-5034
TEL 706-754-5948

LEROY WHEELER PARKER
See pages 51 and 88

SAN FRANCISCO MUSEUM OF ART — SAN FRANCISCO, CA

OAKLAND ART MUSEUM — OAKLAND, CA — 510-839-9997

ZOË PASTERNACK
See page 25

JERSEY CITY, NJ
FAX 201-656-6645
TEL 201-795-3259

THE CLAY POT — BROOKLYN, NY — 718-788-6564

FIRE OPAL — JAMAICA PLAIN, MA — 617-524-0262

TERRA FIRMA — BELMONT, MA — 617-489-5353

SANDPEOPLE — HANALEI, HI — 808-826-7848

OUT OF HAND — SAN FRANCISCO, CA — 415-826-3885

(Listing continues)

THE BIBELOT SHOPS — ST. PAUL, MN — 612-646-5651

ENDLEMAN GALLERY — NEW HAVEN, CT — 203-776-2517

MOON BLOSSOMS & SNOW — WASHINGTON, DC — 202-543-8181

PAT WILIE SCULPTURES
See page 117
PLEASE CONTACT THE ARTIST DIRECTLY

AUSTIN, TX
FAX 512-443-9409
TEL 512-443-1105

THE PHILOSOPHER'S STONE
See page 86

ROSEBUD, NS CANADA
FAX 902-644-3273
TEL 902-644-3273

KAYA KAYA — VANCOUVER, BC CANADA — 604-732-1816

NIJINSKA'S — WINNIPEG, MB CANADA — 204-956-2552

THE GALLERY SHOP — HALIFAX, NS CANADA — 902-424-3003

PHOENIX STUDIOS
See page 116

HARMONY, CA
FAX 805-927-0724
TEL 805-927-4248

TOPEO GALLERY — NEW HOPE, PA — 215-862-2750

DON MULLER GALLERY — NORTHAMPTON, MA — 413-586-1119

PETRI'S — SAUSALITO, CA — 415-332-2225

BALSAM GALLERY — WAYNESVILLE, NC — 704-452-2524

MARK WILLIAMS GOLDSMITH — LEWISBURG, PA — 717-523-7882

ARTIFAX — NORFOLK, VA — 804-623-8840

GLASS REUNIONS — RICHMOND, VA — 804-643-3233

WALTER WHITE GALLERY — CARMEL, CA — 408-624-4957

PLEET COLLECTION
See page 95
PLEASE CONTACT THE ARTIST DIRECTLY

DIX HILLS, NY
FAX 516-385-0798
TEL 516-271-1594

ELIZABETH PRIOR
See page 21

PORTLAND, ME
FAX 207-775-4737
TEL 207-775-4737

THE CLAY POT — BROOKLYN, NY — 718-788-6564

NEAL ROSENBLUM GOLDSMITHS — WORCESTER, MA — 508-755-4244

KATIE GINGRASS GALLERY — MILWAUKEE, WI — 414-289-0855

THE STORE NEXT DOOR — NEW YORK, NY — 212-606-0200

TOMLINSON CRAFT COLLECTION — BALTIMORE, MD — 410-338-1572

FIBULA — PORTLAND, ME — 207-761-4432

TONI PUTNAM
See page 74

GARRISON, NY
FAX 914-424-3123
TEL 914-424-3416

SCULPTURE HOUSE & GARDENS — CARMEL, CA — 408-624-2476

FINDING THE ARTWORK

RAINBOW RUGS BY ROSE
See page 102

HOP BOTTOM, PA
FAX 717-289-4194
TEL 717-289-4538

AMERICAN ACCENTS
TAYLOR, PA
717-562-2449

JUD RANDALL
See page 48
PLEASE CONTACT THE ARTIST DIRECTLY

TAMPA, FL
TEL 813-920-2410

RED WOLF COLLECTION
See page 28

FRANKLIN, NC
TEL 704-369-3880

INSIDE AMERICA
MIAMI, FL
305-371-7354

CELIA AND KEITH RICE-JONES
See page 91

NEW WESTMINSTER, BC CANADA
FAX 604-540-1062
TEL 604-521-7887

TRUDY VAN DOP GALLERY
NEW WESTMINSTER, BC CANADA
604-521-7887

RIVER WEAVING AND BATIK COMPANY
See page 88
PLEASE CONTACT THE ARTIST DIRECTLY

KALAMAZOO, MI
TEL 616-345-3120

RITA RODGERS
See page 31

LENOIR CITY, TN
FAX 423-986-4343
TEL 423-986-4343

ALLANSTAND
ASHEVILLE, NC
704-298-7928

GUILD CRAFTS
ASHEVILLE, NC
704-298-7903

CROSSED PALMS GALLERY
BOKEELIA, FL
913-283-2283

PARKWAY CRAFT CENTER
BLOWING ROCK, NC
704-295-7938

ARROWCRAFT SHOP
GATLINBURG, TN
615-436-4604

BETSY ROSS
See page 44

NEW YORK, NY
FAX 914-679-4780
TEL 914-679-7964

CROSS HARRIS FINE CRAFTS
NEW YORK, NY
212-888-7878

SLEEPING BEAR GALLERY
KETCHUM, ID
208-726-3059

PERIMETER GALLERY
HOUSTON, TX
713-521-5928

THE GOLDEN EGG GALLERY
LAGUNA BEACH, CA
774-376-0063

LAURA ROSS
See page 38

PROSPECT, KY
TEL 502-228-5034

LEFT BANK GALLERY
WELLFLEET, MA
508-349-9451

KENTUCKY ART & CRAFT
LOUISVILLE, KY
502-589-0102

HOADLEY GALLERY
LENOX, MA
413-637-2814

CRAFT COMPANY #6
ROCHESTER, NY
716-473-3413

NEW WEST GALLERY
DURANGO, CO
303-259-5777

ROCHE BOBOIS
PHILADELPHIA, PA
215-972-0168

FIREWORKS GALLERY
SEATTLE, WA
206-282-8707

DETROIT INSTITUTE OF THE ARTS
DETROIT, MI
313-833-3924

ROUX ROUX
See page 72

BROOKLYN, NY
FAX 718-625-0581
TEL 718-875-4858

ZONA
NEW YORK, NY
212-925-6750

EDENSIDE GALLERY
LOUISVILLE, KY
502-459-2787

MCGOWAN & CO.
OAKLAND, CA
510-339-0814

SQUARE ONE
PROVINCETOWN, MA
508-487-0642

IOTA
DALLAS, TX
214-522-2999

SIMONS & GREEN
S. MIAMI, FL
305-667-1692

THE STORE NEXT DOOR
NEW YORK, NY
212-606-0200

RUSS'S RURAL ROCKERS
See page 81
PLEASE CONTACT THE ARTIST DIRECTLY

SPARTA, TN
TEL 615-738-9006

DEBORAH SABO
See page 35

RIVERHEAD, NY
FAX 516-288-0551
TEL 516-369-9225

POSITIVE IMAGES
AUSTIN, TX
512-472-1831

MINDSCAPE
EVANSTON, IL
708-864-2660

THE ZOO GALLERY
FT WALTON BEACH, FL
904-243-6702

AMERICAN ARTISAN, INC
NASHVILLE, TN
615-298-4691

SELDOM SEEN GALLERY
FORT LAUDERDALE, FL
305-522-7556

FIREWORKS GALLERY
SEATTLE, WA
206-282-8707

PIRJO
WASHINGTON, DC
202-337-1390

ICAAN GALLERIES
MANHATTAN BEACH, CA
310-376-6171

RONALD SALOMON
VERGENNES, VT
See page 110   **TEL 800-475-2998**

AMERICAN ORIGINALS	CHARLESTON, SC 803-853-5034
ANDERSON GALLERY	PONTIAC, MI 810-335-4611
STUDIO DESCARTES	MONTREAL, PQ CANADA 514-844-2892
DRESHER GALLERY	LINCOLN CITY, OR 503-994-7342

MICHELE SAVELLE
SEATTLE, WA
See page 56   **TEL 206-233-0433**
PLEASE CONTACT THE ARTIST DIRECTLY

KUNIKATSU SETO
TOKYO, JAPAN
See page 82
PLEASE CONTACT THE ARTIST   **FAX 011-81-3-3400-3201**
c/o YUKO YOKOYAMA, JOMON-SHA   **TEL 011-81-3-3400-3221**

GALLERY QUAI	ISHIKAWA PREF., JAPAN TEL 011-81-768-11-8685
GALLERY ISOGAYA	TOKYO, JAPAN TEL 011-81-3-3591-8797
GALLERY TAO	TOKYO, JAPAN TEL 011-81-3-3403-1190

JULIE SHAW
See page 17

TWIST	PORTLAND, OR 503-224-0334
EDGEWOOD ORCHARD GALLERIES	FISH CREEK, WI 414-868-3579
SUN UP GALLERY	WESTERLY, RI 401-596-0800
THE SPECTRUM	BREWSTER, MA 508-385-3322
AMERICAN PIE	PHILADELPHIA, PA 215-922-2226
CAROL JAMES GALLERY	ROYAL OAK, MI 313-541-6216
STRAWBERRY JAM	NEW HOPE, PA 215-862-9251
ARTISANS THREE	SPRING HOUSE, PA 215-643-4504

MARION PHILIPSEN SHENTON
JOHNSON, VT
See page 106   **FAX 802-635-2731**
    TEL 802-635-2731

COMMON WEALTH GALLERY	LOUISVILLE, KY 502-589-4747
THE PICTURE SHOW	ELKHART, IN 219-294-3166
L. FREUD TITANIUM	BIRMINGHAM, AL 205-320-0980
JULIA RUSH GALLERY	HICKORY, NC 704-324-0409
CARRIBEAN CASTINGS	ST. JOHN, UT 809-693-8520

RICHARD SHEREMETA
DELRAY BEACH, FL
See page 121   **FAX 407-276-7344**
    TEL 407-276-7300

MEREDITH GALLERY	BALTIMORE, MD 301-837-3575

SUSAN M. SIPOS
PHILADELPHIA, PA
See page 40   **TEL 215-482-5681**

OWEN PATRICK GALLERY	PHILADELPHIA, PA 215-482-9395
FUNCTIONAL ART OF VIRGINIA	NORFOLK, VA 800-423-8655
CRAFT COMPANY #6	ROCHESTER, NY 716-473-3413
EXIT ART	LONGBOAT KEY, FL 813-383-4099
MIDLAND CRAFTERS	PINEHURST, NC 910-295-6156
ARTIFACTS	NEW ORLEANS, LA 504-899-5505
PASSING GLIMPSE	LOS ANGELES, CA 310-858-1776
LACOSTE GALLERY	CONCORD, MA 508-369-0278

IRENA STEIN
BURLINGAME, CA
See page 16   **FAX 415-344-9470**
    TEL 415-344-9470

POTTERY A LA CARTE	PITTSFORD, NY 716-264-0770
LUNA	LAGUNA BEACH, CA 14-497-3509
HARMONY POTTERY	HARMONY, CA 805-927-4293
PEOPLE'S POTTERY	ITHACA, NY 607-277-3597
MOON BLOSSOMS & SNOW	WASHINGTON, DC 202-543-8181

SURVING STUDIOS
MIDDLETOWN, NY
See page 49   **FAX 914-355-1517**
    TEL 914-355-1430

CLOUDS GALLERY	WOODSTOCK, NY 914-679-8155
DIAMOND TANITA GALLERY	CRESTED BUTTE, CO 303-349-0940
TAOS BLUE	TAOS, NM 505-758-3561
MACKEREL SKY GALLERY	E. LANSING, MI 517-351-2211
NELLIE BLY	JEROME, AZ 602-634-0255
RIVER GALLERY	CHATANOOGA, TN 615-267-7353
LINDSEY GALLERY	OAK PARK, IL 708-386-5272

TRENT TALLY
FAYETTEVILLE, AR
See page 41   **FAX 501-643-3356**
    TEL 501-643-3314

GALLERY AT TERRA STUDIOS INC.	FAYETTEVILLE, AR 501-643-3314
INTERIORS BY CANOVA	TULSA, OK 918-459-8308
FORT SMITH ARTS CENTER GALLERY	FORT SMITH, AR 501-784-2787
INTERIORS BY CANOVA	FAYETTEVILLE, AR 501-582-5882
INTERIORS BY CANOVA	SPRINGFIELD, MO 417-882-6166
ARKANSAS CRAFT GALLERY	FAYETTEVILLE, AR 501-521-2016
ARKANSAS CRAFT GALLERY	HOT SPRINGS, AR 501-321-1640
ARKANSAS CRAFT GALLERY	EUREKA SPRINGS, AR 501-253-7072

FINDING THE ARTWORK

TOM TORRENS SCULPTURE DESIGN
See page 70

GIG HARBOR, WA
FAX 206-265-2404
TEL 206-857-5831

THE NATURE COMPANY

DISCOVERY CHANNEL STORE

EARTHENWORKS — LA CONNER, WA / 360-466-4422

THE PHOENIX — BIG SUR, CA / 408-667-2347

CLARKSVILLE POTTERY — AUSTIN, TX / 512-454-9079

CLAY PIGEON — SEDONA, AZ / 520-282-2845

NEW MORNING GALLERY — ASHEVILLE, NC / 704-274-2831

WARD & CHILD — SALT LAKE CITY, UT / 801-595-6622

GISELA VON EICKEN
See page 31

NEW YORK, NY
FAX 212-387-8327
TEL 212-780-0840

PEIPERS & KOJAN — NEW YORK, NY / 212-744-1047

MAIN STREET GALLERY — SAG HARBOR, NY / 516-725-9884

AMERICAN CRAFT MUSEUM — NEW YORK, NY / 212-956-3535

NATALIE WARRENS
See page 38

PORTLAND, OR
TEL 503-236-8671

THE CLAY POT — BROOKLYN, NY / 718-788-6564

GIFTED HAND GALLERY — WELLESLEY, MA / 617-235-7171

CRAFT COMPANY #6 — ROCHESTER, NY / 716-473-3413

ACCIPITER — RALEIGH, NC / 919-755-9309

EARTHWORKS — LOS ALTOS, CA / 415-948-5141

LILL STREET GALLERY — CHICAGO, IL / 312-477-6185

ITCHY FINGERS — PORTLAND, OR / 503-222-5237

J.H. WARRINGTON
See page 109

BEAUFORT, SC
TEL 803-524-CATS

SOCIETY OF ARTS & CRAFTS — BOSTON, MA / 617-266-1810

THE EMPORIUM — BLACK MOUNTAIN, NC / 704-669-0050

SEVEN SISTERS GALLERY — BLACK MOUNTAIN, NC / 714-669-5107

SHADY LANE — SALUDA, NC / 704-749-1155

GROVEWOOD GALLERY — ASHEVILLE, NC / 704-253-7651

OAKS GALLERY — DILLSBORO, NC / 704-586-6542

FOLK ART CENTER — ASHEVILLE, NC / 704-298-7928

ARROWCRAFT SHOP — GATLINBURG, TN / 615-436-4604

ALICE WATTERSON
See page 96

SANTA FE, NM
TEL 505-982-1737

SANTA FE WEAVING GALLERY — SANTA FE, NM / 505-982-1737

ISADORA DUNCAN — SEDONA, AZ / 520-282-9487

OBSIDIAN GALLERY — TUCSON, AZ / 602-577-3598

MIND'S EYE GALLERY — SCOTTSDALE, AZ / 602-941-2494

WINNEPESAUKEE FORGE, INC.
See page 116
PLEASE CONTACT THE ARTIST DIRECTLY

MEREDITH, NH
FAX 603-279-4243
TEL 603-279-5492

JIMMY WRAY
See page 125

KEY WEST, FL
TEL 305-296-1811

LILL STREET GALLERY — CHICAGO, IL / 312-477-6185

HARRISON GALLERY — KEY WEST, FL / 305-294-0609

KEY WEST WOODWORKS — KEY WEST, FL / 305-296-1811

JUNKO YAMADA
See page 47
PLEASE CONTACT THE ARTIST
C/o YUKO YOKOYAMA, JOMON-SHA

TOKYO, JAPAN
FAX 011-81-3-3400-3201
TEL 011-81-3-3400-3221

TSUCHI NO HANA GALLERY — TOKYO, JAPAN / TEL 011-81-3-3400-1013

NANCY J. YOUNG AND ALLEN YOUNG
See page 96

ALBUQUERQUE, NM
FAX 505-299-2238
TEL 505-299-6108

LA FUENTE GALLERY — SEDONA, AZ / 602-282-5276

ES POSIBLE GALLERY — SCOTTSDALE, AZ / 602-488-3770

NEW TRENDS GALLERY — SANTA FE, NM / 505-988-1199

KEENE GALLERY — SAN ANTONIO, TX / 210-299-1999

GALLERY A — TAOS, NM / 505-758-2343

WEEMS GALLERY — ALBUQUERQUE, NM / 505-293-6133

LARRY ZGODA
See page 61

CHICAGO, IL
FAX 312-943-9987
TEL 312-943-9978

VALE CRAFT GALLERY — CHICAGO, IL / 312-337-3525

MCMILLAN GALLERY — MADISON, WI / 608-238-6501

LINDSEY GALLERY — OAK PARK, IL / 708-386-5272

GALLERY LISTINGS
A State-by-State Directory

> Each of the nearly 400 galleries listed here carry the work of one or more **Contemporary Craft** artists. Some specialize in certain media, others have a regional or thematic focus, and many can facilitate special orders and projects. The list is a great travel companion and may reveal some unfamiliar galleries in your own backyard.

ALABAMA

L. FREUD TITANIUM
BIRMINGHAM, AL
TEL 205-320-0980

ALASKA

BUNNELL ST. GALLERY
HOMER, AK
TEL 907-235-2662

ARIZONA

BEAD IT!
PRESCOTT, AZ
TEL 520-445-9234

CLAY PIGEON
SEDONA, AZ
TEL 520-282-2845

ES POSIBLE GALLERY
SCOTTSDALE, AZ
TEL 602-488-3770

ISADORA DUNCAN
SEDONA, AZ
TEL 520-282-9487

LA FUENTE GALLERY
SEDONA, AZ
TEL 602-282-5276

LEKAE GALLERIES
SCOTTSDALE, AZ
TEL 602-874-2624

MIND'S EYE GALLERY
SCOTTSDALE, AZ
TEL 602-941-2494

NELLIE BLY
JEROME, AZ
TEL 602-634-0255

OBSIDIAN GALLERY
TUCSON, AZ
TEL 602-577-3598

PHILABAUM GLASS STUDIO
TUCSON, AZ
TEL 602-884-7604

ARKANSAS

ARKANSAS CRAFT GALLERY
HOT SPRINGS, AR
TEL 501-321-1640

ARKANSAS CRAFT GALLERY
EUREKA SPRINGS, AR
TEL 501-253-7072

ARKANSAS CRAFT GALLERY
FAYETTEVILLE, AR
TEL 501-521-2016

FORT SMITH ARTS CENTER GALLERY
FT. SMITH, AR
TEL 501-784-2787

GALLERY AT TERRA STUDIOS
FAYETTEVILLE, AR
TEL 501-643-3314

INTERIORS BY CANOVA
FAYETTEVILLE, AR
TEL 501-582-5882

CALIFORNIA

ACCI
BERKELEY, CA
TEL 510-843-2527

BRANSON BOUTIQUE
KENTFIELD, CA
TEL 415-925-1850

CEDANNA GALLERY & STORE
SAN FRANCISCO, CA
TEL 415-474-7152

CONCEPTS
CARMEL, CA
TEL 408-624-0661

CONCEPTS BY J, INC.
LOS ANGELES, CA
TEL 213-564-9988

COONLEY GALLERY
PALO ALTO, CA
TEL 415-327-4000

DE NOVO
PALO ALTO, CA
TEL 415-327-1256

DEL MANO GALLERY
LOS ANGELES, CA
TEL 310-476-8508

DOLPHIN DREAMS
WALNUT CREEK, CA
TEL 510-933-2342

EARTH SPIRITS
PALM DESERT, CA
TEL 619-779-8766

EARTHWORKS
LOS ALTOS, CA
TEL 415-948-5141

GALLERY ALEXANDER
LA JOLLA, CA
TEL 619-459-9433

GRAPHIC'S GALLERY
BALBOA ISLAND, CA
TEL 714-673-2220

HARMONY POTTERY
HARMONY, CA
TEL 805-927-4293

HUNTER UNLIMITED
SANTA BARBARA, CA
TEL 805-899-0007

ICAAN GALLERIES
MANHATTAN BEACH, CA
TEL 310-376-6171

IMAGE OF THE CULTURE
PALO ALTO, CA
TEL 415-342-0621

JOANNE'S STAINED GLASS
TRUCKEE, CA
TEL 916-587-1280

GALLERY LISTINGS

LEGENDS
SONOMA, CA
TEL 707-939-8100

LUNA
LAGUNA BEACH, CA
TEL 714-497-3509

MCGOWAN & CO.
OAKLAND, CA
TEL 510-339-0814

MEADOWLARK GALLERY
CORTE MADERA, CA
TEL 415-924-2210

MICHAELJON WOODWORKER
CLEMENTS, CA
TEL 209-763-5713

OAKLAND ART MUSEUM
OAKLAND, CA
TEL 510-839-9997

OUT OF HAND
SAN FRANCISCO, CA
TEL 415-826-3885

PASSING GLIMPSE
LOS ANGELES, CA
TEL 310-858-1776

PETRI'S
SAUSALITO, CA
TEL 415-332-2225

RASBERRYS
YOUNTVILLE, CA
TEL 707-944-9211

SAN ANSELMO ART GLASS GALLERY
SAN ANSELMO, CA
TEL 415-457-2082

SAVAS GALLERY
MILL VALLEY, CA
TEL 415-380-8098

SCULPTURE HOUSE & GARDENS
CARMEL, CA
TEL 408-624-2476

SEEKERS COLLECTION & GALLERY
CAMBRIA, CA
TEL 805-927-8626

SOMETHING/ANYTHING
SAN FRANCISCO, CA
TEL 415-441-8003

SPIRALS
PALO ALTO, CA
TEL 415-324-1155

THE GOLDEN EGG GALLERY
LAGUNA BEACH, CA
TEL 774-376-0063

THE IMP
SANTA MONICA, CA
TEL 310-917-3320

THE PHOENIX
BIG SUR, CA
TEL 408-667-2347

VIRGINIA BREIER GALLERY
SAN FRANCISCO, CA
TEL 415-929-7173

WALTER WHITE GALLERY
CARMEL, CA
TEL 408-624-4957

WOLFARD & COMPANY
SANTA ROSA, CA
TEL 707-542-7526

COLORADO

ABBEY LANE GALLERY
CREEDE, CO
TEL 719-658-2736

BRISTOL GALLERY
DENVER, CO
TEL 303-620-9822

DESIGN COLLABORATION
DENVER, CO
TEL 303-825-6353

DIAMOND TANITA GALLERY
CRESTED BUTTE, CO
TEL 303-349-0940

INTERNATIONAL VILLA
DENVER, CO
TEL 303-333-1524

LIMITED ADDITIONS
ASPEN, CO
TEL 970-925-7112

NEW WEST GALLERY
DURANGO, CO
TEL 303-259-5777

SPIRITS IN THE WIND GALLERY
GOLDEN, CO
TEL 303-279-1192

TERMAR GALLERY
DURANGO, CO
TEL 970-247-3728

THE ART OF CRAFT
DENVER, CO
TEL 303-292-5564

THE RACHAEL COLLECTION
ASPEN, CO
TEL 303-920-1313

CONNECTICUT

ENDLEMAN GALLERY
NEW HAVEN, CT
TEL 203-776-2517

GUILFORD HANDCRAFTS, INC.
GUILFORD, CT
TEL 203-453-5947

WAVE
NEW HAVEN, CT
TEL 203-782-6212

DELAWARE

DELAWARE CENTER FOR THE ARTS
WILMINGTON, DE
TEL 302-656-6466

TIDELINE GALLERY
REHOBOTH BEACH, DE
TEL 302-227-4444

TIDELINE GALLERY
GREENVILLE, DE
TEL 302-651-9444

DISTRICT OF COLUMBIA

LIPERT INTERNATIONAL
WASHINGTON, DC
TEL 202-625-0541

MOON BLOSSOMS & SNOW
WASHINGTON, DC
TEL 202-543-8181

PIRJO
WASHINGTON, DC
TEL 202-337-1390

SANSAR GALLERY
WASHINGTON, DC
TEL 202-244-4448

FLORIDA

A PLACE ON EARTH
STUART, FL
TEL 407-283-9556

AMERICAN CRAFTWORKS
BOCA RATON, FL
TEL 407-362-4220

ART UPTOWN, INC.
SARASOTA, FL
TEL 941-955-5409

ARTSI PHARTSI
TAMPA, FL
TEL 813-832-2787

CREATIVE INSPIRATIONS GALLERY
FT. LAUDERDALE, FL
TEL 954-525-1870

CROSSED PALMS GALLERY
BOKEELIA, FL
TEL 913-283-2283

EXIT ART
LONGBOAT KEY, FL
TEL 813-383-4099

GLASS CANVAS GALLERY INC.
SAINT PETERSBURG, FL
TEL 813-821-6767

GRAND CENTRAL GALLERY
TAMPA, FL
TEL 813-254-4977

HARRISON GALLERY
KEY WEST, FL
TEL 305-294-0609

INSIDE AMERICA
MIAMI, FL
TEL 305-371-7354

KEY WEST WOODWORKS
KEY WEST, FL
TEL 305-296-1811

NEWBILL COLLECTION
SEASIDE, FL
TEL 904-231-4500

OVERWHELMED
BOCA RATON, FL
TEL 407-368-0078

SELDOM SEEN
FT. LAUDERDALE, FL
TEL 305-764-5590

SIMONS & GREEN
S. MIAMI, FL
TEL 305-667-1692

THE ZOO GALLERY
FT. WALTON BEACH, FL
TEL 904-243-6702

TIMOTHY'S GALLERY
WINTER PARK, FL
TEL 407-629-0707

VINCENT WILLIAM GALLERY INC.
ST. PETE BEACH, FL
TEL 813-363-1334

GEORGIA

AURUM STUDIOS
ATHENS, GA
TEL 706-546-8826

D. MORGAN GALLERY
CONYERS, GA
TEL 404-922-4554

EDGE OF THE WORLD GALLERY
ATLANTA, GA
TEL 404-249-7752

FRAGILE
ATLANTA, GA
TEL 404-257-1323

ILLUMINA
ATLANTA, GA
TEL 404-233-3010

THE RED DOOR GALLERY
CARROLLTON, GA
TEL 770-830-0025

VESPERMANN GLASS GALLERY
ATLANTA, GA .
TEL 404-350-9698

HAWAII

BEADS OF PARADISE
PAIA MAUI, HI
TEL 808-579-9459

CONTEMPORARY MUSEUM SHOP
HONOLULU, HI
TEL 808-523-3447

SANDPEOPLE
HANALEI, HI
TEL 808-826-7848

IDAHO

SLEEPING BEAR GALLERY
KETCHUM, ID
TEL 208-726-3059

ILLINOIS

ADESSO, LTD
HIGHLAND PARK, IL
TEL 708-433-8525

ANNELEE GALLERY
GLENWOOD, IL
TEL 708-757-7100

ARTISAN'S GALLERY
WILMETTE, IL
TEL 708-251-3775

ARTS AND ARTISANS, LTD.
CHICAGO, IL
TEL 312-855-9220

BEAD IT!
CHICAGO, IL
TEL 312-561-9683

CITY WOODS
HIGHLAND PARK, IL
TEL 708-432-9393

EASTERN ILLINOIS UNIVERSITY
CHARLESTON, IL
TEL 217-581-3410

ECLECTIC JUNCTION
CHICAGO, IL
TEL 312-342-7865

EXPRESSLY WOOD
EVANSTON, IL
TEL 708-869-7060

LILL STREET GALLERY
CHICAGO, IL
TEL 312-477-6185

LINDSEY GALLERY
OAK PARK, IL
TEL 708-386-5272

MARY BELL GALLERIES
CHICAGO, IL
TEL 312-642-0202

MATERIAL POSSESSIONS
CHICAGO, IL
TEL 312-280-4885

MINDSCAPE
EVANSTON, IL
TEL 708-864-2660

PIECES
HIGHLAND PARK, IL
TEL 708-432-2137

SEO GALLERIA
CHICAGO, IL
TEL 312-477-1030

TABULA TUA
CHICAGO, IL
TEL 312-929-5338

THE GOOD WORKS GALLERY
GLEN ELLYNE, IL
TEL 708-858-6654

VALE CRAFT GALLERY
CHICAGO, IL
TEL 312-337-3525

INDIANA

FORT WAYNE MUSEUM OF ART
FT. WAYNE, IN
TEL 219-422-6467

THE PICTURE SHOW
ELKHART, IN
TEL 219-294-3166

IOWA

ELDERBERRY COLLECTION
WEST DES MOINES, IA
TEL 515-271-5045

**OCTAGON CENTER
FOR THE ARTS**
AMES, IA
TEL 515-232-5331

SIGNATURE
WEST DES MOINES, IA
TEL 515-277-5865

KENTUCKY

COMMON WEALTH GALLERY
LOUISVILLE, KY
TEL 502-589-4747

EDENSIDE GALLERY
LOUISVILLE, KY
TEL 502-459-2787

KENTUCKY ART & CRAFT
LOUISVILLE, KY
TEL 502-589-0102

PROMENADE GALLERY
BEREA, KY
TEL 606-986-1609

LOUISIANA

ARTIFACTS
NEW ORLEANS, LA
TEL 504-899-5505

LASTING INDULGENCE
NEW ORLEANS, LA
TEL 504-525-2440

RUMORS
NEW ORLEANS, LA
TEL 504-525-0292

GALLERY LISTINGS

MAINE

ARIES FINE AMERICAN CRAFTS
OGUNQUITI, ME
TEL 207-646-5597

BLUE HERON GALLERY
DEER ISLE, ME
TEL 207-348-6051

FIBULA
PORTLAND, ME
TEL 207-761-4432

HANDWORKS
BLUE HILL, ME
TEL 207-374-5613

HARBOR SQUARE GALLERY
ROCKLAND, ME
TEL 207-594-8700

LEIGHTON GALLERY
BLUE HILL, ME
TEL 207-374-5001

NANCY MARGOLIS GALLERY
PORTLAND, ME
TEL 207-775-3822

SAWYER STREET GALLERY
S. PORTLAND, ME
TEL 207-767-7113

STEIN GALLERY
PORTLAND, ME
TEL 207-772-9072

THOS. MOSER
PORTLAND, ME
TEL 207-774-3791

MARYLAND

GRAND JURY
BETHESDA, MD
TEL 301-530-7982

TMEREDITH GALLERY
BALTIMORE, MD
TEL 301-837-3575

TOMLINSON CRAFT COLLECTION
BALTIMORE, MD
TEL 410-338-1572

ZYZYX
BETHESDA, MD
TEL 301-493-0297

ZYZYX
BALTIMORE, MD
TEL 410-486-9785

MASSACHUSETTS

ALIANZA CONTEMPORARY CRAFTS
BOSTON, MA
TEL 617-262-2385

ARTFUL HAND
BOSTON, MA
TEL 617-262-9601

ARTFUL HAND GALLERIES
ORLEANS, MA
TEL 617-255-2969

BEADWORKS
BOSTON, MA
TEL 617-247-7227

BERTRAM M. COHEN
BOSTON, MA
TEL 617-247-9093

DECOR INTERNATIONAL, INC
BOSTON, MA
TEL 617-262-1529

DON MULLER GALLERY
NORTHAMPTON, MA
TEL 413-586-1119

FIRE OPAL
JAMAICA PLAIN, MA
TEL 617-524-0262

GIFTED HAND GALLERY
WELLESLEY, MA
TEL 617-235-7171

HOADLEY GALLERY
LENOX, MA
TEL 413-637-2814

ICARUS
NEWBURYPORT, MA
TEL 508-463-9246

IMPULSE
PROVINCETOWN, MA
TEL 508-487-1154

LACOSTE GALLERY
CONCORD, MA
TEL 508-369-0278

LE CHERCHE-MIDI
NANTUCKET, MA
TEL 508-228-7600

LEFT BANK GALLERY
WELLFLEET, MA
TEL 508-349-9451

NEAL ROSENBLUM GOLDSMITHS
WORCESTER, MA
TEL 508-755-4244

ORIEL
SOUTH HADLEY, MA
TEL 413-532-6469

SIGNATURE GALLERY
CHESTNUT HILL, MA
TEL 617-332-7749

SIGNATURE STORES INC.
MASHPEE, MA
TEL 508-539-0029

SILVERSCAPE DESIGNS
NORTHAMPTON, MA
TEL 413-253-3324

SOCIETY OF ARTS & CRAFTS
BOSTON, MA
TEL 617-266-1810

SQUARE ONE
PROVINCETOWN, MA
TEL 508-487-0642

STEPHEN FELLERMAN
SHEFFIELD, MA
TEL 413-229-8533

TERRA FIRMA
BELMONT, MA
TEL 617-489-5353

THE SOCIETY OF ARTS & CRAFTS
BOSTON, MA
TEL 617-266-1810

THE SPECTRUM
BREWSTER, MA
TEL 508-385-3322

MICHIGAN

16 HANDS GALLERY
ANN ARBOR, MI
TEL 313-761-1110

ANDERSON GALLERY
PONTIAC, MI
TEL 810-335-4611

ARIANA GALLERY
ROYAL OAK, MI
TEL 810-546-8810

ART GLASS ALCOVE
SAUGATUCK, MI
TEL 616-857-1854

BIER POTTERY
CHARLLEVOIX, MI
TEL 616-547-2288

CAROL JAMES GALLERY
ROYAL OAK, MI
TEL 313-541-6216

DETROIT GALLERY OF CONTEMPORARY
DETROIT, MI
TEL 313-873-7888

DETROIT INSTITUTE OF THE ARTS
DETROIT, MI
TEL 313-833-3924

ILONA AND GALLERY
WEST BLOOMFIELD, MI
TEL 810-855-4488

MACKEREL SKY GALLERY
E. LANSING, MI
TEL 517-351-2211

PERRY SHERWOOD FINE ART
PETOSKY, MI
TEL 616-348-5079

SANDRA COLLINS, INC
BIRMINGHAM, MI
TEL 313-642-4795

THE PAINTED BIRD
SUTTON'S BAY, MI
TEL 616-271-3050

MINNESOTA

ART RESOURCES GALLERY
SAINT PAUL, MN
TEL 612-222-4431

ART RESOURCES GALLERY
EDINA, MN
TEL 612-922-1770

BEAD IT!
BLOOMINGTON, MN
TEL 612-858-8612

CELEBRATION DESIGNS
SAINT PAUL, MN
TEL 612-690-4344

DAVLINS
MINNEAPOLIS, MN
TEL 612-378-1036

MARSHALL FIELD'S
MINNEAPOLIS, MN
TEL 612-307-5871

NORTHFIELD ARTS GUILD
NORTHFIELD, MN
TEL 507-645-8877

THE BIBELOT SHOPS
ST. PAUL, MN
TEL 612-646-5651

THREE ROOMS UP
EDINA, MN
TEL 612-922-7231

MISSOURI

BLUESTEM MISSOURI CRAFTS
COLUMBIA, MO
TEL 314-442-0211

CRAFT ALLIANCE
ST. LOUIS, MO
TEL 314-725-1177

INTERIORS BY CANOVA
SPRINGFIELD, MO
TEL 417-882-6166

MONTANA

ACCENTS WEST
BOZEMAN, MT
TEL 406-586-4185

NEBRASKA

ADAM WHITNEY GALLERY
OMAHA, NE
TEL 402-393-1051

NEW HAMPSHIRE

WINNEPESAUKEE FORGE INC.
MEREDITH, NH
TEL 603-274-5492

NEW JERSEY

CBL FINE ART
WEST ORANGE, NJ
TEL 201-736-7776

ELEANOR'S CRAFT GALLERY
ENGLEWOOD, NJ
TEL 201-816-7376

F. GERALD NEW
MORRISTOWN, NJ
TEL 201-425-4485

TERRY IVORY
STONE HARBOUR, NJ
TEL 609-967-4138

NEW MEXICO

CLAY AND FIBER
TAOS, NM
TEL 505-758-8093

FAIRCHILD & CO.
SANTA FE, NM
TEL 505-984-1419

GALLERY A
TAOS, NM
TEL 505-758-2343

NEW TRENDS GALLERY
SANTA FE, NM
TEL 505-988-1199

OFF THE WALL
SANTA FE, NM
TEL 505-983-8337

SANTA FE WEAVING GALLERY
SANTA FE, NM
TEL 505-982-1737

SOUTHWEST CONTEMPORARY JEWELRY
ALBUQUERQUE, NM
TEL 505-243-1108

TAOS BLUE
TAOS, NM
TEL 505-758-3561

WEEMS GALLERY
ALBUQUERQUE, NM
TEL 505-293-6133

NEW YORK

ADRIEN LINFORD
NEW YORK, NY
TEL 212-628-4500

AFTER THE RAIN
NEW YORK, NY
TEL 212-431-1044

AMALGAMATED
NEW YORK, NY
TEL 212-691-8695

AMERICAN CRAFT MUSEUM
NEW YORK, NY
TEL 212-956-3535

AN AMERICAN CRAFTSMAN
NEW YORK, NY
TEL 212-399-2555

AN AMERICAN CRAFTSMAN
NEW YORK, NY
TEL 212-727-0841

ARTCRAFTERS
BUFFALO, NY
TEL 716-881-4320

ARTISANS ALLEY
NIAGARA FALLS, NY
TEL 716-282-0196

BARNEYS
NEW YORK, NY
TEL 212-339-7300

CASCABEL
SCARSDALE, NY
TEL 914-725-8922

CLOUDS GALLERY
WOODSTOCK, NY
TEL 914-679-8155

CORNING MUSEUM SHOP
CORNING, NY
TEL 607-974-8271

CRAFT COMPANY #6
ROCHESTER, NY
TEL 716-473-3413

CROSS HARRIS FINE CRAFTS
NEW YORK, NY
TEL 212-888-7878

ENGEL GALLERY
EAST HAMPTON, NY
TEL 516-324-6462

GAYLE WILLSON GALLERY
SOUTHAMPTON, NY
TEL 516-283-7430

MAIN STREET GALLERY
SAG HARBOR, NY
TEL 516-725-9884

MARK MILLIKEN GALLERY
NEW YORK, NY
TEL 212-534-8802

MUD SWEAT & TEARS EAST
NEW YORK, NY
TEL 212-570-6868

NEW GLASS GALLERY
NEW YORK, NY
TEL 212-431-0050

PEIPERS & KOJAN
NEW YORK, NY
TEL 212-744-1047

PEOPLE'S POTTERY
ITHACA, NY
TEL 607-277-3597

POTTERY A LA CARTE
PITTSFORD, NY
TEL 716-264-0770

THE CLAY POT
BROOKLYN, NY
TEL 718-788-6564

THE COLLECTOR
MERRICK, NY
TEL 516-379-0805

THE GUGGENHEIM MUSEUM
NEW YORK, NY
TEL 212-423-3500

GALLERY LISTINGS

THE STORE NEXT DOOR
NEW YORK, NY
TEL 212-606-0200

ZONA
NEW YORK, NY
TFI 212-925-6750

NORTH CAROLINA

ACCIPITER
RALEIGH, NC
TEL 919-755-9309

ALLANSTAND
ASHEVILLE, NC
TEL 704-298-7928

BALSAM GALLERY
WAYNESVILLE, NC
TEL 704-452-2524

BROWNING ARTWORK
FRISCO, NC
TEL 919-995-5538

CREATED WITH CLAY
HIGH POINT, NC
TEL 919-841-8792

DANICAARTWEAR
GREENSBORO, NC
TEL 910-271-0871

FIRST LIGHT GALLERY
CHARLOTTE, NC
TEL 704-543-9939

FOLK ART CENTER
ASHEVILLE, NC
TEL 704-298-7928

GALLERY WDO
CHARLOTTE, NC
TEL 704-333-9173

GROVEWOOD GALLERY
ASHEVILLE, NC
TEL 704-253-7651

GUILD CRAFTS
ASHEVILLE, NC
TEL 704-298-7903

HARLLEE GALLERY
HIGHLANDS, NC
TEL 704-526-2083

JULIA RUSH GALLERY
HICKORY, NC
TEL 704-324-0409

MIDLAND CRAFTERS
PINEHURST, NC
TEL 910-295-6156

NEW MORNING GALLERY
ASHEVILLE, NC
TEL 704-274-2831

OAKS GALLERY
DILLSBORO, NC
TEL 704-586-6542

PARKWAY CRAFT CENTER
BLOWING ROCK, NC
TEL 704-295-7938

RAINBOW HARVEST
DUCK, NC
TEL 919-261-5949

SEVEN SISTERS GALLERY
BLACK MOUNTAIN, NC
TEL 714-669-5107

SHADY LANE
SALUDA, NC
TEL 704-749-1155

SOMERHILL GALLERY
CHAPEL HILL, NC
TEL 919-968-8868

THE EMPORIUM
BLACK MOUNTAIN, NC
TEL 704-669-0050

TRILLIUM GALLERY
LITTLE SWITZERLAND, NC
TEL 704-765-0024

OHIO

AVALON GALLERY
ROCKY RIVER, OH
TEL 216-331-3776

**DON DRUMM
STUDIOS & GALLERY**
AKRON, OH
TEL 216-253-6268

DUDA GALLERY
BRECKSVILLE, OH
TEL 216-526-3210

DUNCAN GALLERY
HUDSON, OH
TEL 216-650-6199

**GORDON BEALE
FRANK GALLERY**
CLEVELAND, OH
TEL 216-421-0677

MILLER GALLERY
CINCINNATI, OH
TEL 513-871-4420

OSHER OSHER GALLERY
LYNDHURST, OH
TEL 216-646-9191

RAINBOWERS
HUDSON, OH
TEL 216-467-0259

SILVIA ULLMAN GALLERY
CLEVELAND, OH
TEL 216-231-2008

THE MODERN OBJECT
COLUMBUS, OH
TEL 614-461-9114

OKLAHOMA

INTERIORS BY CANOVA
TULSA, OK
TEL 918-459-8303

OREGON

DRESHER GALLERY
LINCOLN CITY, OR
TEL 503-994-7342

EARTHWORKS GALLERY
YACHATS, OR
TEL 503-547-4300

EXCLUSIVE ACCENTS
MEDFORD, OR
TEL 503-776-1215

ITCHY FINGERS
PORTLAND, OR
TEL 503-222-5237

**THE REAL
MOTHER GOOSE GALLERY**
PORTLAND, OR
TEL 503-223-3737

TWIST
PORTLAND, OR
TEL 503-224-0334

WEBSTERS
ASHLAND, OR
TEL 503-482-9801

WHITEBIRD
CANNON BEACH, OR
TEL 503-436-2681

PENNSYLVANIA

AMERICAN ACCENTS
TAYLOR, PA
TEL 717-562-2449

AMERICAN PIE
PHILADELPHIA, PA
TEL 215-922-2226

ANGELHEART
NEWTOWN, PA
TEL 215-968-1614

ART EFFECTS GALLERY
BALA CYNWYD, PA
TEL 610-668-0992

ARTISANS THREE
SPRING HOUSE, PA
TEL 215-643-4504

DISCOVERIES
MANAGUNK, PA
TEL 215-482-1117

DISCOVERIES
READING, PA
TEL 215-372-2595

EXPRESSIONS GALLERY
YARDLEY, PA
TEL 215-321-7433

GALLERY 500
ELKINS PARK, PA
TEL 215-572-1203

LANGMAN GAllFRY
WILLOW GROVE, PA
TEL 215-657-8333

MARK WILLIAMS GOLDSMITH
LEWISBURG, PA
TEL 717-523-7882

METALWORKS
PHILADELPHIA, PA
TEL 215-625-2640

OWEN PATRICK GALLERY
PHILADELPHIA, PA
TEL 215-482-9395

ROCHE BOBOIS
PHILADELPHIA, PA
TEL 215-972-0168

STRAWBERRY JAM
NEW HOPE, PA
TEL 215-862-9251

THE GALLERY AT CEDAR HOLLOW
MALVERN, PA
TEL 610-640-2787

THE WORKS GALLERY
PHILADELPHIA, PA
TEL 215-922-7775

TOPEO GALLERY
NEW HOPE, PA
TEL 215-862-2750

TOUCHES
PHILADELPHIA, PA
TEL 215-546-1221

TURTLEDOVE
PHILADELPHIA, PA
TEL 215-487-7350

WOODMERE ART MUSEUM
PHILADELPHIA, PA
TEL 215-247-0476

RHODE ISLAND

SUN UP GALLERY
WESTERLY, RI
TEL 401-596-0800

SOUTH CAROLINA

AMERICAN ORIGINALS
CHARLESTON, SC
TEL 803-853-5034

EAST BAY GALLERY
CHARLESTON, SC
TEL 803-723-5567

HARBOUR TOWN CRAFTS
HILTON HEAD, SC
TEL 803-671-3643

LLYN STRONG
GREENVILLE, SC
TEL 803-233-5900

TENNESSEE

AMERICAN ARTISAN, INC
NASHVILLE, TN
TEL 615-298-4691

ARROWCRAFT SHOP
GATLINBURG, TN
TEL 615-436-4604

EXPRESSIONS
WINCHESTER, TN
TEL 800-266-1622

RIVER GALLERY
CHATANOOGA, TN
TEL 615-267-7353

SOHO SOUTH
MEMPHIS, TN
TEL 901-767-7070

TEXAS

ARTISANS FINE CRAFTS GALLERY
AUSTIN, TX
TEL 512-345-3001

CARLYN GALERIE
DALLAS, TX
TEL 214-368-2828

CLARKSVILLE POTTERY
AUSTIN, TX
TEL 512-454-9079

D. HANKO'S
SUGARLAND, TX
TEL 713-980-1023

FREE FLIGHT GALLERY
DALLAS, TX
TEL 214-701-9566

GALLERY GOLDSMITHS
HOUSTON, TX
TEL 713-961-3552

HANSON GALLERIES
HOUSTON, TX
TEL 713-984-1242

HIGH GLOSS
HOUSTON, TX
TEL 713-468-2915

IOTA
DALLAS, TX
TEL 214-522-2999

KEENE GALLERY
SAN ANTONIO, TX
TEL 210-299-1999

KITTRELL/RIFFKIND ART GLASS
DALLAS, TX
TEL 214-239-7957

PERIMETER GALLERY
HOUSTON, TX
TEL 713-521-5928

POSITIVE IMAGES
AUSTIN, TX
TEL 512-472-1831

SABLE V FINE ART GALLERY
WIMBERLEY, TX
TEL 512-847-8975

STUDIO B
FREDERICKSBURG, TX
TEL 210-997-4547

THE OLE MOON
DALLAS, IX
TEL 214-827-9921

VERTU
DALLAS, TX
TEL 214-520-7817

UTAH

CARRIBEAN CASTINGS
ST. JOHN, UT
TEL 809-693-8520

DOUBECK & DOUBECK STUDIOS
SALT LAKE CITY, UT
TEL 801-487-1410

PLEASURES
PARK CITY, UT
TEL 801-649-5733

WARD & CHILD
SALT LAKE CITY, UT
TEL 801-595-6622

VIRGINIA

AMERICAN ARTISAN INC
ALEXANDRIA, VA
TEL 703-548-3431

APPALACHIAN SPRING
FALLS CHURCH, VA
TEL 703-533-0930

ARTIFAX
NORFOLK, VA
TEL 804-623-8840

ARTS AFIRE GLASS GALLERY
ALEXANDRIA, VA
TEL 703-838-9785

FISHSCALE & MOUSETOOTH
MANASSAS, VA
TEL 703-330-1263

FUNCTIONAL ART OF VIRGINIA
NORFOLK, VA
TEL 800-423-8655

GLASS REUNIONS
RICHMOND, VA
TEL 804-643-3233

GALLERY LISTINGS

WASHINGTON

EARTHENWORKS
LA CONNER, WA
TEL 360-466-4422

FIREWORKS GALLERY
SEATTLE, WA
TEL 206-682-8707

HIGH SPIRITS
WENATCHEE, WA
TEL 509-633-7798

MESOLINI & AMICI
SEATTLE, WA
TEL 206-587-0275

MIA GALLERY
SEATTLE, WA
TEL 206-467-8283

PHOENIX RISING GALLERY
SEATTLE, WA
TEL 206-728-2332

RAGAZZI'S FLYING SHUTTLE
SEATTLE, WA
TEL 206-343-9762

THE GLASS EYE
SEATTLE, WA
TEL 800-237-6961

UNDERCOVER QUILTS
SEATTLE, WA
TEL 206-622-6382

WEST VIRGINIA

STUDIO 40
WHITE SULPHUR SPRINGS, WV
TEL 304-536-4898

WISCONSIN

ACCENTRICS LTD
MEQUON, WI
TEL 414-241-9292

ATYPIC GALLERY
MILWAUKEE, WI
TEL 414-351-0333

EDGEWOOD ORCHARD GALLERIES
FISH CREEK, WI
TEL 414-868-3579

**GWENDOLYN'S
AT WHISTLING SWAN**
FISH CREEK, WI
TEL 414-868-3602

JOHNSTON GALLERY
MINERAL POINT, WI
TEL 608-087-3787

KATIE GINGRASS GALLERY
MILWAUKEE, WI
TEL 414-289-0855

KOHLER ARTS CENTER
KOHLER, WI
TEL 414-452-8602

LITTLE LUXURIES
MADISON, WI
TEL 608-255-7372

MADISON ART CENTER
MADISON, WI
TEL 608-257-0158

MAPLE GROVE GALLERY
FISH CREEK, WI
TEL 414-839-2693

MCMILLAN GALLERY
MADISON, WI
TEL 608-238-6501

CANADA

KAYA KAYA
VANCOUVER, BC, CANADA
TEL 604-732-1816

MOUNTAIN CRAFT GALLERY
WHISTLER WAY, BC, CANADA
TEL 604-932-5001

THREE GRACES INC.
VANCOUVER, BC, CANADA
TEL 604-254-4212

TRUDY VAN DOP GALLERY
NEW WESTMINSTER, BC, CANADA
TEL 604-521-7887

NIJINSKA'S
WINNIPEG, MB, CANADA
TEL 204-956-2552

THE GALLERY SHOP
HALIFAX, NS, CANADA
TEL 902-424-3003

STUDIO DESCARTES
MONTREAL, PQ, CANADA
TEL 514-844-2892

JAPAN

GALLERY ISOGAYA
TOKYO, JAPAN
TEL 011-81-3-3591-8797

GALLERY QUAI
TOKYO, JAPAN
TEL 011-81-768-22-8685

GALLERY TAO
TOKYO, JAPAN
TEL 011-81-3-3403-1190

KI NO AKARI GALLERY
YONEZAWA, YAMAGATA PREF.
JAPAN
TEL 011-81-238-23-9376

SUYA GALLERY
KYOTO, JAPAN
TEL 011-81-75-211-7700

TSUCHI NO HANA GALLERY
TOKYO, JAPAN
TEL 011-81-3-3400-1013

SWITZERLAND

REFLECTIONS GLASS GALLERY
GENEVA, SWITZERLAND

SELECTED ORGANIZATIONS & PUBLICATIONS

PUBLICATIONS

AMERICAN CERAMICS

9 E 45 ST #603
NEW YORK, NY 10017
FAX 212-661-2389
TEL 212-661-4397

$28/year

American Ceramics, an art quarterly, was founded to enhance the preservation of ceramics' rich heritage and to document contemporary developments in the field. Articles feature the best and brightest ceramists: rising stars and established luminaries, as well as those early pioneers who transformed ceramics into a genuine art form.

Recent articles include:

Dishing Out the Fantasies: Viola Frey's Ceramic Plates

From the Pedestal to the Wall: Works on Paper by Betty Woodman

Ugo Nespolo and the Art of Majolica

AMERICAN CRAFT

AMERICAN CRAFT COUNCIL
72 SPRING ST
NEW YORK, NY 10012-4019
FAX 212-274-0650
TEL 212-274-0630

$40/year

American Craft, a bimonthly magazine, focuses on contemporary craft through artist profiles, reviews of major shows, a portfolio of emerging artists, a national calendar and news section, and book reviews, as well as illustrated columns reporting on commissions, acquisitions and exhibitions.

Recent articles include:

Danforth Pewterers: A Proud Family Tradition Lives On in the Vermont Mountains

Twentieth-Century Jewelry at the Oakland Museum

The Making of Quilts; The Maker of Quilts

CERAMICS MONTHLY

PROFESSIONAL PUBLICATIONS, INC.
1609 NORTHWEST BLVD
PO BOX 12788
COLUMBUS, OH 43212-0788
FAX 614-488-4561
TEL 614-488-8236

$22/year

Ceramics Monthly offers a broad range of articles—including artist profiles, reviews of exhibitions, historical features, and business and technical information—for potters, ceramic sculptors, collectors, gallery and museum personnel, and interested observers.

Recent articles include:

Residential Tile

The Lowly Bean Pot

Raku Potter Charles Bohn

THE CRAFTS REPORT

300 WATER ST
PO BOX 1992
WILMINGTON, DE 19899
FAX 302-656-4894
TEL 302-656-2209
TEL 800-777-7098

$29/year

Published monthly, The Crafts Report seeks to inform, instruct and inspire both the beginning and the established professional craftsperson, as well as the crafts retailer, by providing them with business articles, industry news and a forum for exchanging ideas and concerns.

Recent articles include:

Interior Design and Crafts

Galleries and Artists: A Delicate Alliance

Nine Steps to Networking with the Power Brokers in Your Town

FIBERARTS

50 COLLEGE ST
ASHEVILLE, NC 28801
FAX 704-253-7952
TEL 704-253-0467
TEL 000-281-3388

$21/year

Five annual issues of Fiberarts focus on contemporary textile art, including clothing, quilts, baskets, paper, tapestry, needlework and surface design. Features include artist profiles, critical essays, book reviews, and extensive listings of opportunities, events and resources.

Recent articles include:

From a Gallery Owner's Perspective: An Interview with Louise Allrich

Playing With a Full Deck: Elements That Identify Contemporary Art Quilts of the 1990s

New Voices in Weaving: Cynthia Schira Looks at the Next Generation of Weavers

FINE WOODWORKING

THE TAUNTON PRESS, INC.
PO BOX 5506
NEWTOWN, CT 06470-5506
FAX 203-426-3434
TEL 203-426-8171

$29/year

Fine Woodworking is a bimonthly magazine for all those who strive for and appreciate excellence in woodworking — veteran professional and weekend hobbyist alike. Articles by skilled woodworkers focus on basics of tool use, stock preparation and joinery, as well as specialized techniques and finishing.

Recent articles include:

Thomas Braverman Blends Old World into New Work

A Hall Table Both Traditional and Contemporary

Patternmaker's Vices

SELECTED ORGANIZATIONS & PUBLICATIONS

GLASS ART

TRAVIN INC.
PO BOX 260377
HIGHLANDS RANCH, CO 80163-0377
FAX 303-791-7739
TEL 303-791-8998

$24/year U.S.

Glass Art, published bimonthly, includes business articles geared towards glass retailers and professional studios, as well as features on hot and cold glass techniques and artist profiles.

Recent articles include:

Provoking Thought and Challenging Tradition

Kliszewski Shard Vessels — Bob Kliss

The Architectural Glass of Arthur Stern

GLASS MAGAZINE

THE GLASS WORKSHOP
647 FULTON ST
BROOKLYN, NY 11217
FAX 718-625-38898
TEL 718-625-3685

$28/year

Glass Magazine, a full-color quarterly for design professionals, artists and collectors, features profiles of contemporary artists, an educational directory, and critical reviews of national and international exhibitions.

Recent articles include:

Conversation: Geraldine Rudge Interviews Oliver Watson, Head of Glass and Ceramics at the Victoria and Albert Museum

Josiah McElheny: The Art of Authentic Forgery

Eve Andrée Laramée: Faith and Reason, Function and Fiction

HOME FURNITURE

THE TAUNTON PRESS, INC.
63 S MAIN ST
NEWTOWN, CT 06470-5506
FAX 203-426-3434
TEL 203-426-8171
TEL 800-888-8286

$20/year

Home Furniture, a new, full-color quarterly magazine, is both a portfolio of top contemporary furniture makers and a review of furniture design. Articles include artist profiles and discussions of furniture history and design.

Recent articles include:

Old Forms, New Furniture

CAD as a Design Tool

English Origins of Arts and Crafts

METALSMITH

5009 LONDONDERRY DR
TAMPA, FL 33647
FAX 813-977-8462
TEL 813-977-5326

$26/year

Metalsmith, a four-color quarterly, includes artist profiles, critical essays, and reviews. Its focus is on contemporary metal artists producing jewelry, small sculpture and objects. Metalsmith is published by the Society of North American Goldsmiths. Subscription includes a complimentary issue of a special publication, often an Exhibition in Print.

Recent articles include:

Intimate Parallels Between Installation and Wearable Art

Beyond Tradition: The Silver of Bernadette Rodriguez-Caraveo

The Museum: Metals and Collecting for the Future

ORNAMENT

PO BOX 2349
SAN MARCO, CA 92079-2349
FAX 619-599-0228
TEL 619-599-0222

$26/year

Ornament, a full-color quarterly publication, focuses on personal adornment with an emphasis on jewelry, beads and clothing. Features include profiles of contemporary artists; discussions of ancient and ethnic personal adornment; a calendar of events; critical reviews of books, videos and exhibitions; a calendar of events; and articles of technical and historic information.

Recent articles include:

The Creative Instinct: Nancy Chappell

Jewelry Art by Ron Ho, Honolulu Academy of Arts

The Body as Metaphor: Jung Hoo Kim

PSG'S GLASS ARTIST

28 S STATE ST
NEWTOWN, PA 18940
FAX 215-860-1812
TEL 215-860-9947

$25/year

PSG's Glass Artist is a full-color bimonthly publication featuring articles on the creative use of the glass arts and crafts. In addition to how-to information and artist and studio profiles, each issue contains book reviews, career tips, a home-studio section, and a complete calendar of glass-related events.

Recent articles include:

The New Glass Mosaics

Every Glass Picture Tells a Story

Do the Nineties Belong to U.S. Glass?

SURFACE DESIGN JOURNAL

SURFACE DESIGN ASSOCIATION
PO BOX 20799
OAKLAND, CA 94620
FAX 707-829-3285
TEL 510-841-2008

$45/year

Surface Design Journal, a full-color quarterly magazine, is published by the Surface Design Association (SDA), a nonprofit educational organization of artists, educators, designers, and lovers of beautiful textiles and quality design. Subscription to the Surface Design Journal is provided as a benefit of membership in the SDA.

Recent articles include:

Printed Matters: Two Perspectives on Designing for Industry

On CAD and Its Possibilities: An Appraisal of Computer-Aided Design

2010: A Millennial Perspective

WOODSHOP NEWS

SOUNDINGS PUBLICATIONS, INC.
35 PRATT ST
ESSEX, CT 06426
FAX 203-767-1048
TEL 203-767-8227

$15.97/year

Woodshop News, published monthly, includes features and descriptions about new technology, artists and their techniques, trade news and source information.

Recent articles include:

Sam Maloof: Legendary Craftsman Continues Building Legacy of Fine Furniture

Galleries Feature Array of Furniture From Found Wood to Chinese Antiques

One Cottage Street Woodworker Adds Panache to Tradition

ORGANIZATIONS

AMERICAN ASSOCIATION OF WOODTURNERS

3200 LEXINGTON AVE
SHOREVIEW, MN 55126-8118
FAX 612-484-1724
TEL 612-484-9094

Mary Redig, Administrator

The American Association of Woodturners (AAW) is a non-profit organization dedicated to the advancement of woodturning. Seventy-nine chapters throughout the United States provide education and information for those interested in woodturning. Members include hobbyists, professionals, gallery owners, collectors, and wood and equipment suppliers.

AMERICAN CRAFT COUNCIL

72 SPRING ST
NEW YORK, NY 10012-4006
FAX 212-274-0650
TEL 212-274-0630

Hunter Kariher, Executive Director

The American Craft Council (ACC) stimulates public awareness and appreciation of the work of American craftspeople through museum exhibitions and educational programs, visual aids and publications. The American Craft Museum is an affiliate of the ACC; membership is shared.

The ACC consists of four operating units:

1. American Craft Enterprises produces exhibitions of handmade objects made by America's most talented craftspeople to enhance the awareness of American craft and to provide the opportunity for the public to acquire such crafts;

2. American Craft Publishing produces a bimonthly magazine to enhance the understanding and appreciation of American crafts;

3. American Craft Association produces educational seminars and audio-visual materials to educate craftspeople, and provides support services for craftspeople;

4. American Craft Information Center provides information on American crafts through a book/exhibit catalog collection and unique files on American craftspeople.

AMERICAN SOCIETY OF FURNITURE ARTISTS

PO BOX 7491
HOUSTON, TX 77248-7491
FAX 713-556-5444
TEL 713-556-5444

Adam St. John, President

The American Society of Furniture Artists (ASOFA) is a non-profit organization dedicated to the field of 'art furniture' and to the artists who create it. Organized in 1989, ASOFA is the only national organization of such artists. The Society's nationwide scope promotes the highest professional standards and provide its members with significant avenues for continued artistic and professional development.

AMERICAN TAPESTRY ALLIANCE

128 MONTICELLO RD
OAK RIDGE, TN 37830
TEL 423-483-0772

Marti Fleischer, President

The American Tapestry Alliance was founded in 1982 to: (1) promote an awareness of and an appreciation for tapestries designed and woven in America; (2) establish, perpetrate and recognize superior quality tapestries by American tapestry artists; (3) encourage greater use of tapestries by corporate and private collectors; (4) educate the public about tapestry; and (5) coordinate national and international juried tapestry shows, exhibiting the finest quality American-made works.

CREATIVE GLASS CENTER OF AMERICA

1501 GLASSTOWN ROAD
PO BOX 646
MILLVILLE, NJ 08332-1566
FAX 609-825-2410
TEL 609-825-6800

The Creative Glass Center is a public attraction devoted to increasing know-how of glass works. The Creative Glass Center of America offers insight to glass arts through the Museum of American Glass, an informational resource center providing fellowships; demonstrations in the T.C. Wheaton Glass Factory; and various tours throughout Wheaton Village.

THE EMBROIDERERS' GUILD OF AMERICA, INC.

335 W. BROADWAY #100
LOUISVILLE, KY 40202
FAX 502-584-7900
TEL 502-589-6956

Jeanette Lovensheimer, President

The Embroiderer's Guild of America (EGA) seeks to set and maintain high standards of design, color and workmanship in all kinds of embroidery and canvas work. EGA sponsors lectures, exhibitions, competitions and field trips; offers examinations for teaching certification; and serves as an information source for needlework in the United States. EGA also maintains a comprehensive reference library for research and study, and publishes *Needle Arts,* a quarterly magazine.

GLASS ART SOCIETY

1305 FOURTH AVE #711
SEATTLE, WA 98101-2401
FAX 206-382-2630
TEL 206-382-1305

Alice Rooney, Executive Director

The Glass Art Society (GAS), an international non-profit organization, was founded in 1971 to encourage excellence and advance appreciation, understanding and development of the glass arts worldwide. GAS promotes communication among artists, educators, students, collectors, gallery and museum personnel, art critics, manufacturers and others through an annual conference and through the *Glass Art Society Journal* and newsletters.

HANDWEAVERS GUILD OF AMERICA, INC.

2402 UNIVERSITY AVE W #702
ST. PAUL, MN 55114-1701
FAX 612-646-0806
TEL 612-646-0802
E-MAIL to Compuserve 73744.202

Marcy Petrini, President

The Handweavers Guild of America, Inc. (HGA) is an international non-profit organization dedicated to upholding excellence, promoting the textile arts, and preserving our textile heritage. HGA provides a forum for education, opportunities for networking, and inspiration and encouragement for handweavers, handspinners and related fiber artists. HGA publishes a quarterly journal for members, *Shuttle, Spindle & Dyepot.*

SELECTED ORGANIZATIONS & PUBLICATIONS

INTERNATIONAL TAPESTRY NETWORK

PO BOX 203228
ANCHORAGE, AK 99520-3228
FAX 907-346-3316
TEL 907-346-2392

Helga Berry, President

International Tapestry Network (ITNET) is a not-for-profit global network of tapestry artists, teachers, curators and collectors. ITNET works to develop greater awareness of contemporary tapestry as an art form by sponsoring international tapestry exhibitions and by educating the public and encouraging dialogue about tapestry on an international level. ITNET publishes a quarterly newsletter, distributed worldwide. Newsletter correspondents and advisory board members search for and share news of exhibitions, educational opportunities and other tapestry events.

NATIONAL COUNCIL ON EDUCATION FOR THE CERAMIC ARTS

PO BOX 158
BANDON, OR 97411
TEL 503-347-4394
TEL 800-99N-CECA

Regina Brown, Executive Secretary

The National Council on Education for the Ceramic Arts (NCECA) is a professional organization of individuals whose interests, talents, or careers are primarily focused on the ceramic arts. NCECA strives to stimulate, promote and improve education in the ceramic arts, and to gather and disseminate information and ideas that are vital and stimulating to teachers, studio artists and others throughout the creative studies community. NCECA hosts a national conference each spring.

NATIONAL WOODCARVERS ASSOCIATION

PO BOX 43218
CINCINNATI, OH 45243
TEL 513-561-0627

Edward F. Gallenstein, President

The National Woodcarvers Association (NWCA) promotes woodcarving and fellowship among its members; encourages exhibitions and area get-togethers; publishes *Chip Chats*, a bi-monthly magazine, and assists members in finding tool and wood suppliers, as well as markets for their work. Many distinguished professional woodcarvers in the United States and abroad share their know-how with fellow members.

SOCIETY OF AMERICAN SILVERSMITHS

PO BOX 3599
CRANSTON, RI 02910-0599
FAX 401-461-3196
TEL 401-461-3156
TEL 800-584-2352
E-MAIL SLVRSMITH@AOL.COM

Jeffrey Herman, Executive Director

The Society of American Silversmiths (SAS) was founded in 1989 to preserve the art and history of contemporary handcrafted holloware, flatware and sculpture. SAS also provides its juried artisan members with support, networking and greater access to the market, partly through its annual traveling exhibitions. The public is welcome to consult SAS with all silver-related questions, including those regarding silversmithing techniques, history and restoration. A unique referral service commissions work from artisan members for collectors, corporations and museums.

SOCIETY OF NORTH AMERICAN GOLDSMITHS

5009 LONDONDERRY DR
TAMPA, FL 33647
FAX 813-977-8462
TEL 813-977-5326

Bob Mitchell, Executive Administrator

The Society of North American Goldsmiths (SNAG) was founded in 1970 to promote contemporary metalwork and jewelry. Through its publications, services and advocacy, the Society serves the fine art and jewelry communities with publications and conferences for members, practitioners and teachers of metalwork. Professional metalsmiths, students, collectors, gallery owners and enthusiasts form the dynamic mix of the Society.

SURFACE DESIGN ASSOCIATION

PO BOX 20799
OAKLAND, CA 94620
FAX 707-829-3285
TEL 510-841-2008

Joy Stocksdale, Administrator

The Surface Design Association promotes surface design through education, encouragement of individual artists, communication of technical information and information concerning professional opportunities, and the exchange of ideas through conferences and publications.

INDEX OF ARTISTS AND COMPANIES